THE THEOLOGICAL DEFENSE OF PAPAL POWER
BY
SAINT ALPHONSUS DE LIGUORI

This dissertation was conducted under the direction of Reverend Alfred A. Rush, C.SS.R., M.A., S.T.D. as major professor, and was approved by Reverend Eugene Burke, C.S.P., S.T.D., and Reverend John Shinners, S.T.D., as readers.

THE CATHOLIC UNIVERSITY OF AMERICA
STUDIES IN SACRED THEOLOGY
No. 119

The Theological Defense of Papal Power

By St. Alphonsus de Liguori

ABSTRACT OF A DISSERTATION

*Submitted to the Faculty of the School of Sacred Theology
of the Catholic University of America in Partial
Fulfillment of the Requirements for the
Degree of Doctor of Sacred Theology*

BY

DAVID JOHN SHARROCK, C.SS.R., S.T.L.

THE CATHOLIC UNIVERSITY OF AMERICA PRESS
WASHINGTON, D. C.
1961

Imprimi Potest:

    James Connolly, C.SS.R., J.C.D.

    Prov. Sup.

Nihil Obstat:

    Rt. Rev. Wilfrid W. Nash

    Censor Librorum

Imprimatur:

    John M. Gannon

    Archbishop - Bishop of Erie

    Erie, March 1, 1961

Copyright, 1961
by
THE CATHOLIC UNIVERSITY OF AMERICA

Printed by
MAC-DIL ASSOCIATES, INC.
1802 Parade Street
Erie, Pennsylvania

THE THEOLOGICAL DEFENSE OF PAPAL POWER
BY
SAINT ALPHONSUS DE LIGUORI

TABLE OF CONTENTS

FOREWORD   vi

CHAPTER ONE:
    An historical background to the writings of St. Alphonsus on Papal Authority.   1

CHAPTER TWO:
    The writings of St. Alphonsus on Papal Authority   48

CHAPTER THREE:
    St. Alphonsus' Concept of Papal Authority.   75

CHAPTER FIVE:
    St. Alphonsus' use of the Magisterium to establish Papal Authority.

  Part One:
    An evaluation of St. Alphonsus' Use of the Magisterium   92

Abbreviations used in the bibliography and in the footnotes   121

Bibliography   123

Table of Contents of Complete Dissertation   136

FOREWORD

In 1870, the Vatican Council by its Constitution, <u>Pastor Aeternus</u> defined the nature of the power which the Roman Pontiff possesses. The very next year, Pope Pius IX declared St. Alphonsus de Liguori a Doctor of the Church and singled out Alphonsus' defense of the rights of the Apostolic See.

The Council in defining the Pope's rights and powers declared that it based its teaching on the word of God both written and handed down as it had been constantly understood and interpreted by the Church herself. In the history of the Church, there have been many defenders of these rights and powers of the Pope. They, too have drawn their defense from the teachings of Sacred Scripture and the Fathers, and ultimately from the teaching of the Church herself, expressed in the declarations of the Popes and General Councils. St. Alphonsus was one of these defenders whose defense of the Pope by an appeal to the traditional teaching of the Church came at a time when the Pope's God-given rights were being vehemently attacked.

It is the purpose of this work to study St. Alphonsus's theological defense of papal power in that milieu -- a defense which gave the Vatican Council the testimony and thought of still one more of the Church's theologians -- a defense which was so appreciated by the Church that it declared Alphonsus Maria de Liguori <u>Doctor Ecclesiae</u>.

The writer takes this opportunity to thank sincerely all those who have helped him in this work. Deserving of first and special mention is Father Alfred A. Rush, C.SS.R. of the School of Sacred Theology of Catholic University. Father Rush's constant aid and inspiration made this work possible. The writer also wishes to thank Father Eugene Burke, C.S.P. and Father John Shinners who read this work and made many helpful suggestions. Finally, the writer expresses his sincere thanks to his many confreres who showed interest in his work especially to Father Francis Connell, and Father Francis Meehan, and to his major superiors who gave him the opportunity to take graduate work in the School of Sacred Theology at Catholic University of America.

CHAPTER I

AN HISTORICAL BACKGROUND
TO THE WRITINGS OF
ST. ALPHONSUS ON PAPAL AUTHORITY

To understand the writings of a man, it is necessary to know the tenor of the writer's time. No man writes or thinks in a vacuum. His thinking and writing is and must be influenced by the social, political, philosophical, and theological environment of his day. St. Alphonsus de Liguori, whose whole life was bound up in his age as a lawyer, a priest, a teacher, and Bishop is certainly no exception to this general rule. His writings are bound up and intimately concerned with the problems of his age. Thus his ascetical writings[1] treat and defend a sensible asceticism against the rigorous Jansenistic tendencies which had not been entirely crushed in his time. His moral writings[2] defend the liberty of conscience against the rigors of the Jansenists on the one hand, and on the other hand defend the rights of law against the laxism which was beginning to appear as a reaction to Jansenism. In the field of dogmatic theology, one of the great evils of the day was a denial of papal authority. Hence, St. Alphonsus, realizing that a denial of papal supremacy would spell ruin to Christ's Mystical Body on earth, wrote strongly in defense of this papal power.[3] It will be the task of this introductory chapter to show the general anti-papal tendencies which were prevalent in St. Alphonsus' time (he lived from 1696-1787) and then to show the specific anti-papal tendencies with which he had to contend in his own kingdom of Naples.

Endemic to the Church ever since the time of Constantine's conversion to Christianity in 312 has been the great problem of Caeseropapism.⁴ As Philip Hughes puts it: "Caesar is no sooner converted than, as the protector of the things that are God's, he threatens to overshadow the hierarchy and its traditional chief . . . When the first Christian rulers appear . . . the Church . . . meets the problem of Caesaro-papism that has never since ceased to vex her."⁵ Once this basic problem of the relation between the Pope and the Emperor arose, there arose from it many other problems akin to it: What is the relation between the Pope and the nation,⁶ the Pope and his people, the Pope and the Bishops, the Pope and a General Council?⁷ This is not the place to attempt even a brief outline of Caesero-papism and the other problems and questions it suggested. Suffice it to say that the roots of anti-papalism in St. Alphonsus' own day were indeed deep roots, for they had had many centuries in which to grow. The specific anti-papalism with which Alphonsus had to contend can be summed up under four headings, each of which had influence on the other: Absolutism combined with Nationalism, Gallicanism (greatly influenced and developed in an atmosphere of Conciliarism), Jansenism (as allied with Gallicanism) and Febronianism.

In the not too far future, Absolutism and Nationalsim would find many causes to break from one another. At the time of St. Alphonsus, however, the two were united in some sort of peaceful alliance. Absolutism was reaching its peak, and Nationalism was still in the process of growth.⁸ It had not yet reached the stage where it would see Absolutism as one of its

2

greatest enemies.[9] Hence, the problem which faced the papacy at the time of St. Alphonsus were the absolute monarchs in fiercely nationalistic states. In such an atmosphere, the papacy was constantly harrassed and hampered. For Nationalism, with its fierce love, almost adoration, of the civil authority would brook no interference in its internal affairs from any foreign potentate, no matter what claims he might have on its subjects. And the absolute monarchs, who had reverted to the theories of Roman Law and even further developed them, who were firmly convinced of the principle quod principi placuit, legis habet vigorem, would scarcely be willing to acknowledge the validity of any other authority in their domains except their own. Thus, in a nation which regarded itself as almost semi-divine, headed by a man who ruled with divine right, papal authority could be exercised only with the greatest of difficulty.[10]

During the lifetime of St. Alphonsus, the so-called ancien-regime prevailed throughout the whole of continental Europe. The ruler, be he emperor, king, or duke, was in reality monarch, a single personal ruler, untrammelled by any effective parliamentary control. England alone had a constitutional monarchy whereby the king ruled, subject to control of Parliament or minister. Thus, speaking broadly, in the time of St. Alphonsus, all Europe was ruled by absolute monarchs, looking on themselves, and looked on as holding their title to unrestricted rule by divine right. This Absolutism reached its highest peak in the Bourbon dynasties, who ruled not only France, but also Spain and Naples.[11]

These absolutist ideas and ambitions of princes and national monarchs, which were already much in evidence at the opening of the sixteenth century, were forwarded by the religious revolts during this same century. By confiscation of church lands, by appropriation of powers hitherto exercised by the Pope, and by establishment of effective control over the local clergy, the Tudor Sovereigns in England, the kings in Scandinavia, and the German princes, were enriched in purse, and exalted in public opinion. At the same time they were freed from the fear of being hampered in their absolutist policies by an independent ecclesiastical authority. In Catholic countries also, the monarchs took advantage of the Pope's difficulties to wring from him concessions which resulted in shackling the church to the crown.[12] Thus, for example, in France, the Concordat of Bologna in 1516 between Pope Leo X and Francis I secured for the French monarch appointment of bishops and practically a control of benefices within his country -- powers which German princes and English kings secured by revolution. In Spain and Portugal, too, the monarchs obtained concessions from the Pope like those accorded the French sovereigns. They gained a large measure of power over the Church within their countries, and found this power a most valuable ally in forwarding their absolutist tendencies.[13]

  Somewhat later, in the time of St. Alphonsus, the Pope was still according privileges to Catholic Kings. Thus, Benedict XIV (1740 - 1758) in order to protect and promote the interests of the Church by the aid of loyal Catholic Rulers, granted the Kings of Portugal the right of presentation of all sees and abbeys in the Kingdom. To the King of Spain, the Pope gave the right to present the greater part of the benefices, and also the right to place an income tax on the revenues of the clergy. The King of Sardinia received the title of Vicar of the Holy See. This carried with it the rights of nomination to all Church benefices in his dominions and the right to the income of the pontifical fiefs comprised within these same limits.[14] Such concessions merely furthered the designs of the absolute monarchs whose ambitions were to make of the Church a purely national organization totally under their individual control.

So great were some of the concessions to the Catholic monarchs, that Jean Solarzano Pereira (1575-1655) had the boldness to state in his <u>De Indiarum Jure</u>, that in virtue of the bulls at the end of the sixteenth century, all the charge of directing the affairs of the Catholic Church in the Indies fell to the king, making of the king a veritable vicar of the Roman Pontiff who was able to transfer into lay hands the care of ecclesiastical affairs.[15]

Thus, as the divine right of the Pope was denied or flouted, the divine right of kings was asserted and insisted upon. This doctrine of royal absolutism and the divine right theories found their greatest crystallization in the kingdom of France under Louis XIV (1643-1715), guided and directed by his noted Bishop, Bossuet.[16] Carlton Hayes has summed up well Bossuet's theory of government. He writes:

> Government, according to Bosseut, is divinely ordained in order that men may satisfy the God-given natural instincts of living together in organized political society. Under God, monarchy is, of all forms of government, the most usual and the most ancient, and therefore the most natural. It is likewise the strongest and most efficient, therefore the best. It is analogous

5

to the rule of a family by the father, and, like that rule, should be hereditary. Four qualities are referred by the eloquent Bishop to such an hereditary monarch.

1: He is sacred, because he is anointed at the time of coronation by the priests of the Church, and hence it is blasphemy and sacrilege to assail the person of the king or to conspire against him.
2: He is, in a very real sense, the father of his people, the paternal king, and therefore it belongs to him to provide for the welfare of the nation.
3: His power is absolute and autocratic, and for its exercise he is accountable to God alone; no man on earth may rightfully resist the royal commands, and the only recourse for subjects against an evil king is to pray God that his heart be changed.
4: Greater reason is given to a king than to anyone else; the king is an earthly image of God's majesty, and it is wrong, therefore, to look on him as a mere man. The king is a public person and in him the whole nation is embodied. 'As in God are united all perfection and every virtue, so all the power of all the individuals in a community is united in the person of the king.'[17]

Perhaps one of the finest definitions of Absolutism has been given by M. Declareuil:

Absolutism consists in identifying with the State, considered as an entity, the whole national existence. There is nothing which does not emanate from the State, or at least which can exist without the State's permission; it alone creates and founds; nothing can continue to exist unless it retains the favor of the State; having created it, it can destroy. The State absorbs or holds in check all the activities of other bodies, both setting them in motion and reaping the benefits that accrue therefrom. Since absolutism is identical with the omnipotence of the State and excludes the existence of independent institutions outside it, the constitutional form of the State matters but little.[18]

This is absolutism in its fullness. No longer is a monarch necessary but the State as State is supreme and absolute. Whether the State is incarnate in one person, or in several associated organs which only possess sovereignty when combined into one whole is inconsequential. The power of the State remains untouched -- it remains absolute.[19]

With such ideas rampant, it would be inconceivable to any monarch of St. Alphonsus' time to think that he would have to take orders from the Pope -- a foreign sovereign, or that his subjects would have to obey the Pope even despite a contrary command of his own. Such would be tantamount to admitting that he -- the absolute sovereign -- would not have complete control over his own person or over the person of his subjects. Hence, any authority which the Pope would claim that would limit or interfere with the absolute authority claimed by the monarch would be vehemently denied and opposed.

In the light of what has been said, Gallicanism can be seen simply as the particular application of absolutist ideas to the relations of Church and State. Gallicanism can be defined as the complexus of theories, developed in

France, during the latter part of the seventeenth century especially, which, while accepting the Papacy as of divine institution, tends to minimize the papal claims as they have been made in history. It is of two kinds: episcopal, or theological, and political or royal.[20] Episcopal or theological Gallicanism is concerned with those theories which would tend to increase the independence of the French National Church and lessen papal authority over it. Thus, measures were taken in France to increase the authority of the national Assembly of the Bishops, and proportionately decrease the authority of the Pope over the Bishops and the French Church. Royal or national Gallicanism is concerned with those theories which would give the monarch and the nation powers over the Church which would in turn decrease the powers of the Pope. Sometimes the two forms of Gallicanism were in agreement with each other, and sometimes not. Episcopal Gallicanism found justification for its theories in the Councils of Constance (1414-1417) and Basle (1417-1439),[21] while royal Gallicanism appealed to the Pragmatic Sanction of Bourges (1438) and the Concordat of Bologna (1516) for its justification.[22]

    The Council of Constance, not having a head since the beginning of March (1415) (when the anti-Pope, designated as John XXIII had fled to Schaffhausen and retracted there the promises he had made to the Council), on March 29th of that same year drew up the famous four articles of the Council of Constance.[23] The first two are of interest to this study because of their influence on episcopal or theological Gallicanism. First: the Council legitimately convened in the Holy Spirit, is a general Council, represents the Church militant, and has its authority immediately from God, and every person, whatever his dignity, even the Pope, is bound to obey it in all things which pertain to faith, to the extirpation of schism, and to the reform of the Church in both the head and the members. Second: All, even the Pope, who refuse obedience to the decrees and decisions of this Council or of any general Council legitimately convened, are subject to ecclesiastical punishment, and if necessary to other civil penalties.[24]

The Council of Basle did not add too much to these decrees of Constance. It proclaimed in its eleventh session (April 27, 1433) the superiority of a general Council over the Pope.[25] On June 16th of the same year, it declared that it is an article of Faith that the Pope is subordinate to a general Council, and Eugene is a heathen and a publican when he refuses obedience to the Council.[26] Because of the exigencies of the time, Eugene IV did "declare and decree" that the Council was lawful, and he withdrew the decree of dissolution which he had previously issued. He furthermore recognized the Council of Basle as ecumenical from the beginning, and granted that it be continued. In this Bull of December 15, 1433, he omitted the condition he had insisted upon in all earlier declarations, namely, that all the decrees against him and his cardinals be withdrawn.[27] In recognizing the council as ecumenical, he, of course, did not explicitly accept the thesis of the superiority of a council over the pope. Yet, his silence concerning this question did give to it at least an apparent and implicit recognition.[28] Granting the exigencies of the time, perhaps what Eugene IV did was the most prudential thing he could have done. But this apparent implicit recognition did raise havoc with the true claims of papal authority. For it gave the many proponents of Conciliarism and of Gallicanism, and of the general diminution of papal authority, a strong peg on which they could hang their ideas.[29]

The Pragmatic Sanction of Bourges of 1438 was naturally in favor of the superiority of the Council to the Pope, and was opposed to papal reservations and provisions in the collation of benefices. By it, the King claimed the right to recommend his nominees, so that after a time, the kings took the place of the Pope in respect to the major part of the beneficiary and fiscal rights in the national Churches.[30] The Concordat of Bologna (1516) which attempted a compromise between the claims and demands of the Pragmatic Sanction and the rights of the Holy See gave the King of France the right to nominate men to the metropolitan churches, the Cathedrals, the monasteries, and the conventual priories of France.[31]

The Concordat of Bologna, though it did not effect an ideal situation, was a fine stroke of diplomacy on the part of the Holy See, and, as a stop-gap measure, did halt the progress of heresy in France, and at least slowed down the decadence of the clergy in that kingdom.[32] Yet it was an abuse of this Concordat by Louis XIV which gave rise to the final crystallization of the Gallican theories in France. The Concordat had given the king of France the right to exact the revenues of certain vacant bishoprics in France as regalia. King Louis XIV, ignoring this Concordat, claimed the right to the revenues of all the vacant sees.[33] The dispute with Rome which arose over this abuse of the Concordat led to the formulation of the Four Gallican Articles by the Assembly of the French Clergy in 1682. Louis had called this Assembly for the express purpose of having it decide the dispute over the regalia in his favor and draw up a formal declaration of the Gallican theory.[34]

Previous to this, the Faculty of the Sorbonne in 1663 had drawn up a list of six articles which were the immediate forerunners of the Gallican articles. They were formulated in reaction to the theses of Lawrence Desplantes and Gabriel Drouet, which defended papal supremacy. Desplantes defended the universal jurisdiction of the Pope over the whole Church, both in the internal and external forum. Drouet taught that Peter and his successors have authority over the whole Church, that the Popes have given privileges to certain Churches, e.g., the privileges of the Gallican Church, and that although Councils are useful, they are not absolutely necessary.[35] In denial of these claims, the theological Faculty of the Sorbonne held that:

1. It is not a teaching of the Faculty that the Supreme Pontiff has any authority in temporals over the Most Christian King. Indeed, the Faculty has always opposed those who recognize in the Pontiff even a merely indirect authority in such temporals.

2. It is a teaching of the same Faculty that the Most Christian King neither recognizes nor has any superior other than God in temporal matters.

3. It is a teaching of the Faculty that the subjects of the Most Christian King so owe to him fealty and obedience that under no pretext can they be absolved from them.

4. The Faculty declares that it does not approve, and that it has never approved any propositions which are opposed to

the authority of the Most Christian King, or to the canons received in the Kingdom, e.g., that the Pontiff can depose a Bishop in contradiction to these canons.

5. It is not the teaching of the Faculty that the Supreme Pontiff is superior to a General Council.

6. It is not a teaching or a dogma of the Faculty that the Supreme Pontiff is infallible without the assent of the Church to his declarations.[36]

With such principles as a foundation, Bossuet drew up the famous Four Articles of 1682 and presented them to the Assembly of the French Clergy for approbation. These new articles were the articles of the Faculty of the Sorbonne, now expressed in positive form. With these, Louis XIV could put an end to all claims of the Popes who might threaten to excommunicate and depose him.[37] They were in substance:

1. Neither the Pope nor the Church has any power over temporal rulers, and kings cannot be deposed by spiritual authorities, nor can subjects be released from their oath of allegiance.

2. As stated by the Council of Constance, papal power is limited by General Councils.

3. The exercise of papal power is limited by the customs and privileges of the Gallican Church.

4. Although the Pope has the chief voice in

questions of faith, yet his decision is not unalterable unless the consent of the Church is given.[38]

In an Edict of March 22, 1682, Louis XIV approved the Four Articles and imposed them on all France.[39] Pope Innocent XI protested against these articles and in a papal brief of April 11, 1682, Paternae Caritatis, he annulled the acts of the Assembly of 1682.[40] Moreover, he refused to give canonical investiture to priests promoted to bishoprics if they had taken part in the Assembly of 1682, so that in a few years, over thirty-five bishoprics were vacant.[41] Alexander VIII continued the resistance and again declared the Four Articles null and void.[42] The French bishops, fearing a schism, signed a retraction of the articles in 1692.[43] Then, finally in 1693, Louis XIV in a letter to the new Pope, Innocent XII, rescinded his edict of 1682 commanding the enforcement of the articles.[44] The Pope in return yielded on the question of the regalia, and at least a theoretical peace had been reached -- theoretical, for in actual fact, the Four Gallican Articles remained as the expression of the Gallican theory and spread over Europe in spite of papal condemnations. They continued to be taught in seminaries and were held by many of the clergy.[45]

As Gallicanism spread in the other countries of Europe, it differed from country to country in practice and in doctrine. Spanish Gallicanism, for example, was manifested in an increasing use of the Inquisition for political rather than for religious purposes. Genoa and Savoy recalled their ambassadors from Rome. Parma refused to allow money to be sent to the Holy See. In all the countries, the divine origin of the princely power was taught, and the

Pope was held to be only the elected head of the Church, limited like any constitutional monarch.[46] Most historians would agree that one of the major causes for the expulsion of the Jesuits from the Catholic nations of Portugal, France, Spain, Naples, and Parma even before their official suppression by Clement XIV in 1773 was their strong defense of papal supremacy.[47]

Since the tenets of Gallicanism had such an influence on St. Alphonsus' motives for writing his works in defense of papal authority, it would be well to see a summation of its basic teachings as held by a man of Alphonsus' own day. Dom Jamin, a Maurist Benedictine, in 1768 published a popular work called <u>Pensees Theologiques relatives aux Erreurs du Temps</u> which sums up both the French thought, and the general thought on Gallicanism. Dom Jamin held, of course, that the Church is a visible society, and that it alone possesses the marks of the Church of Christ, ie., one, holy, catholic, and apostolic. Jesus Christ is the Supreme Head of this Church, and the Roman Pontiff is the ministerial head, as the successor of St. Peter.[48] He goes on to say that the form of ecclesiastical government is not a democracy, nor an aristocracy, for those who govern are not equal in authority. Nor is it a monarchy, because the authority does not reside in one single person. It is rather, he says, a monarchy tempered by aristocracy, which recognizes one Head whose power is limited by the canons. This head is the Roman Pontiff who has the primacy of honor and jurisdiction. It is up to him to make sure that the canons of the Church are obeyed by the whole Christian world, to call General Councils, and to excommunicate those who refuse to attend. As the Father of all Christians, he can make laws, but they do not have the force of general laws until they have been accepted by the Bishops of the world. For the Bishops are Bishops by divine right holding their power immediately from Jesus Christ, and not from the Pope whose equals they are except in the primacy, which was established by Christ only to show forth unity. And they judge with him in matters of faith and discipline.[49] With regard to the relations between Church and State, Dom Jamin insists upon a mutual independence, and says that the union of the two powers can never be on the principle of subjection of the one to the other. Each, he says, is sovereign, independent, and absolute in its own sphere. Hence, to attribute to the King primacy in ecclesiastical matters is to reverse the order which God has established, and to subject the power of pastors in its exercise to the temporal power is to misunderstand the power of the pastors. On the other hand, the King in the civil and temporal order, has no superior on earth. Thus, to attribute to the Pope a direct or even an indirect power over the temporal power of the King is a doctrine unknown by the Fathers of the first centuries. Following from this, Dom Jamin, of course, rejects the deposing power of the Popes.[50]

Then Dom Jamin goes into the infallible teaching power of the Church. He first claims it for the Church and then goes on to state that infallibility in dogmatic judgements has been given only to the body of Bishops, and that no particular Bishop, not even the Bishop of Rome, may claim this privilege for himself alone. Hence, to maintain that the right of judging cases which concern the faith belongs only to the Pope, and that they should be carried to the Pope or the Holy See in the first instance is a pretension unknown to all antiquity. He says that the Church can pronounce on Faith in many ways: by a general

Council; by a particular Council when the whole Church approves the decision; by the Pope when the moral unanimity of the body of Bishops accepts his judgment; and finally, by the local Bishop who condemns an error in his diocese, if the censure becomes known and is not condemned by the Bishops of the world. A general Council, he states, lawfully assembled, holds its authority directly from God, and all, even the Pope, must be subject to it, for it is the organ of the Holy Spirit. But general Councils are not absolutely necessary in order that the Church decide on some teaching or condemn some error. For even without a Council, the Church, dispersed, but united in the approving of a doctrine or the condemning of an error merits from all her children, complete submission.[51]

Finally, Dom Jamin treats of the obedience which in his opinion should be shown to a papal bull. He states that to propose a bull to the faithful as having of its own nature the power to bind all to obey, or to propose it as containing a doctrine conformable to the Church are two entirely different things. The first is to profess papal infallibility which was entirely unknown to the early Fathers, and also to destroy the rights of the episcopate and reduce the Bishops to the simple role of executors of the decrees of Rome. The second case professes the true doctrine, i.e., one does not owe an entire and unreserved submission to the Pope's judgements, unless they have to do with things of faith and have been assented to by the Bishops scattered throughout the world. It is in this latter sense, says Dom Jamin, that the Church of France demands submission to the constitutions of the Sovereign Pontiff.[52]

From what has been said, it is obvious that the principles of Conciliarism had great influence on the doctrines of Gallicanism.⁵³ Although these principles were widely used during the time of the Great Schism of the West and in the Councils of Constance and Basle, still they were not new principles at this time. True, the exigencies of the time gave them great impetus, but the basic principles of the conciliar theory had been present for a good number of years. Even before Philip the Fair's historic battle with Boniface VIII (1294-1303), at least the theories of Conciliarism had been discussed.

Historians see these theories present in the debates of the canonists in the early 1100's when these men discussed the relation between the Pope and the Church in their more basic discussions on the relation between the monarch and the people of a kingdom.⁵⁴ Moreover, there is a canon in the Decree of Gratian (composed in the early 1100's) which laid down that although normally a Pope was immune from human judgement, this immunity did not extend to a Pope who became a heretic.⁵⁵

H. X. Arquilliere in his treatment of this question, cites various pronouncements in Pope Innocent III's sermons (Innocent reigned from 1198-1216) to show that this canon from the Decree of Gratian reflected an orthodox and established tradition in the Church. He then goes on to describe how this loop-hole was skilfully used by Nogaret in the time of Boniface VIII. Nogaret was able to confuse and almost persuade the prelates of France of the truth of his position in the Assembly of 1303, since the charges of heresy brought against the Pope were technically admissible in Canon Law. Arquilliere says that there was no claim at this time that the Council was superior to a true Pope, since in the case of heresy, the Pope would cease to be Pope. Nevertheless, the very assumption that a General

Council was competent at least to pronounce upon the orthodoxy of a Pope encouraged the growth of a more extreme doctrine of conciliar supremacy. This more extreme doctrine was first explicitly proclaimed by the Spiritual Franciscans in the court of Louis of Bavaria (1314-1330).[56] Hence, when the Gallicans came to use the theories of Conciliarism, they had the advantage of employing principles which had been discussed and developed through many years.[57]

While Gallicanism was developing into the full-blown theory of the Assembly of the French Clergy in 1682, the Church was facing still another crisis also rampant in France, especially. This was the heresy of Jansenism, many times condemned, many times revived. St. Alphonsus met up with this heresy in many different ways. He met it as a Moral theologian, an Ascetic theologian, and also as a Dogmatic theologian and polemicist. It is his contact with Jansenism as a dogmatician and polemicist that is of special interest to this work. The Jansenists, in order to protect themselves from the many papal condemnations, made the famous distinction between de droit and de fait. Such a distinction denied in practice the infallibility of the Pope in defining and settling questions of faith and morals. St. Alphonsus, who opposed Jansenism as an erroneous ascetic and moral doctrine, also opposed it in his dogmatic and polemic works as an antipapal doctrine. It is only insofar as Jansenism was an anti-papal force that it will be outlined here.

It was inevitable that the theories of Jansenism should run afoul the authority of the Holy See, and just as inevitable that the Holy See should finally condemn such doctrines. The Bull of Pope Innocent X, the famous Cum Occasione, on May 31, 1653, condemned the five propositions of the <u>Augustinus</u> written by Cornelius Jansenius and published posthumously by his friends and followers in 1640.[58] This was not the first condemnation of the Jansenists, nor would it be the last, but the previous condemnations had not been accepted on one excuse or another.[59] The subtleties which the Jansenists used to get out from under condemnations were indeed some of the most ingenious in history. It was by a subtlety that the Jansenists tried to avoid the condemnation of their doctrines in the <u>Cum Occasione</u>. In the development of this subtlety, the Jansenists first expressed their anti-papal theories.[60] Doctor Antoine Arnauld, the intellectual leader of Jansenism after the death of St. Cyran in 1643, held that all must accept the condemnation of the five propositions since they had been legitimately condemned by the Church which was infallible in matters of faith. But, he claimed, these propositions were not contained in the book of Jansenius. They were the inventions of Nicholas Cornet. Hence, one did not have to follow the Church on this, because the judgement of whether or not certain things are contained in any specified book does not fall under her infallible power.

    Arnauld thus held that ecclesiastical judgments are not all of equal value, and do not entail the same obligations. Where there is question of the truth or falsity of a doctrine, of its revealed origin or its heterodoxy, the Church, in virtue of its Divine mission is qualified to decide; it is a matter of right. But if the doubt bears upon the presence of this doctrine in some book, this is a question of purely human fact, which, as such, does not fall under the jurisdiction of the supernatural teaching authority instituted in the Church by Jesus Christ. In the former case, once the Church has pronounced judgement, one must conform his belief to its decision. In the latter case, the Church's word should not be openly contradicted. It claims from us the homage of a respectful silence. Yet it does not demand internal assent.[61] This distinction between right and fact was to be the basis of the Jansenist's resistance to papal authority from this time on.

Such a distinction denies papal infallibility with regard to all dogmatic facts, and makes infallibility an almost useless prerogative. For although the Church is infallible in defining a revealed truth, it would not have the power to protect that truth by stating that its contrary is contained in some particular writing.

In other of his writings, Arnauld hits again and again at papal infallibility in dogmatic facts. In his defense of Jansenius against the accusation of heresy, he starts from the principle that the question was not whether his teaching had been previously condemned by the Bull against Baius, or by the Council of Trent, but whether or not it was the teaching of St. Augustine.[62] Thus St. Augustine, not the infallible Magisterium of the Church, is made the norm of orthodoxy. In a response to the Bishop of Alet who attacked his distinction between <u>de droit</u> and <u>de fait</u>, Arnauld writes that the most he can show to a statement of fact made by the Holy See is respectful silence. Otherwise, he would have to admit this "absurd" principle: One is obliged to believe all that the Pope teaches even those things where everyone knows that the Pope is fallible, and those things where one is personally convinced that he is wrong. One would have to do this rather than accept what one knows to be true from certainly convincing proofs which he posesses. To do this, states Arnauld, is to deny the very reason which God has given to man. No one, he says, can command a person who is convinced of the truth of a statement to give up that statement simply in deference to the authority of the Pope. This is to abuse the reason which God has given us.[63]

To the penchant for distinctions for which the Jansenists were famous, must be added one factor which helped forge Jansenism into a formidable anti-papal foe. This factor was Gallicanism. Had not the Jansenists joined forces with the Gallicans, they never would have become the force they did become. (The Gallicans also became a greater power, because of their union with the Jansenists.) Once Jansenism became allied with Gallicanism, then the Holy See had the very delicate problem of stamping out a heresy which had at least somewhat successfully identified itself with the liberties and privileges which the Gallican Church had so long demanded from the Holy See. Thus Jansenism had maneuvered itself into the position of identifying every attack against itself as an attack against the Gallican liberties.

Pastor cites the following case as an example of how intimately and successfully the Jansenists had linked their cause to that of the Gallicans: With a view to investing a new anti-Jansenist Bull[64] with the prestige of the highest legal court in France, the Assembly of the clergy demanded its registration with Parliament. Parliament assented, but in view of the Gallican-Jansenist sentiments of many of the members, there were many difficulties and obstacles raised to its registration. This strong bloc of the Parliament would not tolerate any expression in the act of registration which would have been too favorable to the Pope. Finally, after the King himself demanded its registration, it was so done, but not before Gallicanism had secured a fresh triumph in a fiery speech of Talon, the Advocate-General, in which Talon lowered the dignity and authority of the Holy See and exalted that of the King.[65] The Faculty of the Sorbonne also submitted to the Bull, but only insofar as it concerned the sphere of faith. If it was even suspected that the Pope was trying to intervene in any other sphere but the sphere of faith, Gallican susceptibilities were at once aroused.[66] Thus, Jansenism had found a powerful ally when it joined forces with Gallicanism.

The Papal brief of February 12, 1703, in which Pope Clement XI gave a definitive settlement on the famous cas de conscience[67] brought up another example of the relation between the Jansenists and the Gallicans, and the strength which the Jansenists gained from such a union. D'Aguesseau, the Chancellor of France at the time, has this to say of the reception of the papal brief into the Kingdom:

> Our Liberties do not merely prevent us from accepting laws which are contrary to our customs, but also from having any laws other than our own on matters which regard questions of public order and discipline. Any action initiated by a foreign power within this realm must always be suspect, even though it appears entirely innocent. Thus, the papal brief may be, if you will, a just ordinance, necessary and conducive to peace in the Church, but it is at the same time, the work of a foreign power which has no immediate authority among us in any matters which have to do with public order and discipline. This is sufficient reason for declining to accept it.[68]

As the eighteenth century wore on, the

Jansenists found that even the shelter of ecclesiastical Gallicanism was becoming precarious. For the enemies of their concept of <u>gratia efficax</u> were growing among the Gallicans, and many of the Gallican Bishops were finding it more and more to their advantage to condemn and harass the Jansenists.[69] If the Jansenists were to survive, they needed to ally themselves with an even stronger anti-papal position. They found such a position in the teachings of Edmund Richer. Richer had been chosen by the Faculty of Theology at Sorbonne to get rid of the ultramontanist ideas which were filtering into the School. He developed a theory which did indeed destroy any ultramontanism, and also gave the Jansenists a solid anti-papal position in which to entrench themselves.[70] Briefly, Richer's theories were these:

1. The Church's government has only the outward appearance of a monarchy. In reality it is aristocratic.

2. Legislative power as well as infallibility are not the attributes of the Pope. They belong to the hierarchy composed of the Bishops and the priests, which functions in its totality at a general Council.

3. The Pope is absolutely subject to the Council.

4. The episcopate is an essential element of the constitution of the Church. The papacy is only an accessory.

5. Christ gave to His Church only spiritual means for the attainment of her object.

Hence, the Pope may only make use of spiritual means, never of material force.

6. As the natural guardian of his domains, the prince has both the right and the duty to decide whether the executive ministers of the Church proceed according to the Canons. For such judgements, he is responsible to God alone."[71]

If the Jansenists could convince the clergy and the people of France to accept such theories, they might never fear any real rapprochement with the papacy which would spell their total condemnation and ruin. Thus, they became strong advocates of these theories, and as such, were a powerful anti-papal force with which the Church had to contend.

It was inevitable that the Gallican ideas so rampant in France, Spain, and the small Italian kingdoms should ultimately gain strength in the German kingdoms. For it was greatly to the princes' advantage in the Germanies to espouse the Gallican ideas and to seek the greatest possibile freedom from Rome. It was also to the very great advantage of the spiritual princes, the Bishops, the Archbishops, and the Cardinals, that they, too, be independent of Roman authority. Thus, both political and ecclesiastical Gallicanism found willing ears in the kingdoms of Germany. The princes wished to be absolute masters of every institution in their domain, and the spiritual princes wished to rule their provinces without any interference from Rome. The Bishops deeply resented the interference of the papal nuncios and the dispensations which the nuncios issued. For they felt that they themselves had the power to issue all dispensations in their dioceses. They also resented the heavy contributions from their revenues which the Holy See demanded. There was, as a matter of fact, in the mind of many a German bishop the dream of a German National Church.[72]

The build-up of an anti-papal spirit among both the temporal and spiritual rulers of the Germanies was bound one day to be concretized and synthesized in the work of some German author. With the background of Machiavelli, Sarpi, Richer, Van Espen and many other anti-papal writers, plus this anti-papal spirit, the temptation to gather all these factors into one masterful work would one day captivate the mind of some German Synthesist. Unfortunately for the Church, the mind that was finally captivated was the mind of one of her own Bishops, the Auxiliary of Treves, Nicholas von Hontheim, a contemporary of St. Alphonsus, who lived from 1701-1790. According to Pastor, von Hontheim received his most lasting impressions when a university student at Louvain which Bernard Van Espen had made into one of the strongholds of Gallican and Jansenist teaching. From Louvain, von Hontheim went to Leyden where the new political science of absolutism held sway.[73]

Thus Nicholas von Hontheim had a good background for the work he would write which would sum up so well all the anti-papal, Gallican, and absolutist theories of the day. This work of von Hontheim was, according to Pastor, the book which caused the outbreak of an ecclesiastical crisis which, as far as the inner life of the Church was concerned, was settled only by the Vatican Council.[74] Von Hontheim called his work: <u>Justini Febronii Juris consulti de Statu Ecclesiae et legitima potestate Romani Pontificis Liber singularis ad reuniendos</u>

<u>dissidentes in religione Christiana compositus</u>.[75]
It was first published in September, 1763, by the firm of Esslinger in Frankfort.[76] To protect himself against any condemnatory action by the Holy See, von Hontheim used the pseudonym of Justin Febronius.[77]

This work by von Hontheim was over 700 pages in length. Hence, any summary of this thought must necessarily be only the barest outline of his position. Very briefly, von Hontheim or Febronius taught that:

1. The original character of the Church was not monarchial. This monarchial character was evolved by the successors of St. Peter with the aid and the authority of the False Decretals. Actually, the power of the keys was entrusted by Christ to the whole Church, to be exercised by the prelates, among whom the Pope comes first. But the Pope is subordinate to the Church as a whole.[78]

2. The papal primacy is indeed of Divine institution, but the Pope does not have universal episcopacy, nor universal jurisdiction. Nor does he have the charism of infallibility. These belong to the college of Bishops collectively. The Pope exercises merely the right of surveillance over the whole Church to assure the integrity of the faith; to judge certain cases which are given to him by the Canons; and to convoke general Councils. (However, the Pope does not have the exclusive right to convoke Councils. If he will not call a general Council, the right devolves upon the secular princes). The Pope's position in the Church, therefore, as head of

the Church, is of an administrative and unifying character.[79]

3. The general Council is superior to the Pope. It alone possesses the right to issue binding doctrinal decisions to the whole Church. It is always lawful to appeal from the Pope to a general Council.[80]

4. The word of the Pope has no more value than the word of any other Bishop.[81]

5. It was only by a violation of justice that questions which were at one time left to the decision of provincial synods and metropolitans gradually came to be reserved to the Holy See.[82]

6. The Pope, Bishops, priests, princes, theologians, and canonists are to help restore the genuine constitution of the Church as outlined in the work. But the greatest hope for this restoration lies in the princes of state. For the prince is the sovereign and protector of the Church in his state. As sovereign, he has the power to exercise his <u>regium placet</u> to ban and resist any and all papal decrees which may be harmful to the good harmony of the state. As the protector, the prince is the guardian of the true Church, and in this position, he is raised, in actual practice, above the Pope and Bishops.[83]

Knowing the regalist and Gallican background of the courts of Europe, one can imagine how enthusiastically this work of Febronius was received. Its reception was overwhelming and, according to Pastor, revealed at a stroke all the silent antipathy for the Roman Curia which had established itself in courts and governments, in universities and literary circles.[84] The work was rapidly circulated through many of the European countries. In Spain, the Council of Castile provided for reprints of the book by granting state subsidies. In Portugal, the book was cited in a royal edict against the Jesuits, and a Bishop who wrote a letter to his flock against Febronius was imprisoned. In France translations were made in 1766 and 1777. In Venice, an edition appeared which had the approval of the Senate, and the Italian translation received a thirty year privilege in that kingdom. The Duke of Modena banished his librarian Zaccaria for publishing his Antifebronius in 1767.[85] The Austrian government gave its approval of Febronius' work and placed Zaccaria's Antifebronius on its index of forbidden books. And in the Hapsburg Netherlands, the work had the protection of the highest state authorities.[86]

Febronius' work was condemned and placed on the Index by a decree of February 27, 1764.[87] Moreover, on May 14 of that same year, Pope Clement XIII sent papal briefs to the prelates of Germany asking them to proceed against the work.[88] But the briefs were not well received in the Germanies. In many cases, it was only after much hesitation that the prohibition of the book was even published. And the Elector of Treves refused to dismiss von Hontheim once it was found out that he was Febronius.[89]

Finally, after much discussion, Febronius formally retracted in 1778 and died in union with Rome. But this did not put an end to the influence of his work. Marie-Therese refused to allow the retraction into her kingdom, and a few years

later at Ems in 1786, the Electors (i.e., the
Bishops of Cologne, Mainz and Treves) adopted
the principles of Febronius and attempted to
put them into effect. In a document known as the
<u>Punctuation of Ems</u>, they upheld Febronius'
teachings in twenty-three articles.[90]

The <u>Punctuation of Ems</u> recommended
three successive courts of instance for all ecclesiastical processes: the first, the official
diocesan court; the second, the metropolitan
court; the third and final court of appeal, recourse to German Bishops named by the Pope
to judge the case. It also demanded that all
exemption from episcopal authority enjoyed by
the convents and monasteries be suppressed,
and that the quinquennial faculties be given <u>in
perpetuum</u> (since the powers granted in the
faculties belonged to the Bishops by right of
office, and Rome had no right to reserve these
powers to herself in the first place). It denounced the granting of benefices which had
been usurped by the Pope, the abuses of taxes
for the Roman court, and the requirement of
letters of grace. It went on to state that papal
bulls and briefs have no force for prelates unless they are freely accepted by the prelates.
Finally, the rapport between the Church of
Germany and the Holy See is to be ruled by the
decrees of the Council of Basle, by the Diet of
Mainz, and in a certain measure by the Council
of Vienne.[91]

This meeting of the Electors of Ems was
held just one year before St. Alphonsus died and
eighteen years after he had written his work
against Febronius.[92] It is noted here to show
how far the principles of men like Febronius
could be extended even by Bishops of the Church.
Such an anti-papal spirit could well mean the
destruction of the whole Church. Of this, St.

Alphonsus was very much aware. It was the inevitable extremes of such principles that so frightened him. In a letter to Don Giulio Selvaggio, the Ecclesiastical censor for the Kingdom of Naples, St. Alphonsus expressed these fears. He wrote:

> . . . With regard to the supreme power of the Sovereign Pontiff, I am ready to lay down my life in defense of that doctrine. Take that away, and I assure you the authority of the Church is at an end.[93]

And Febronius did very much to take this supreme power of the Pope away. It was his principles which gave greater life and background to the Punctuation of Ems, to its Italian counterpart, the Synod of Pistoia held in 1786,[94] to Josephism,[95] and to the other anti-papal movements in the European countries. With this work, the absolutist rulers of the eighteenth and nineteenth centuries had a weapon, skilfully fashioned, with which to halt the "encroachments" of the Holy See and the Roman Pontiffs on their domains and on their authority.

From this brief summary, one can see that the general European climate in which St. Alphonsus lived and wrote was an anti-papal, anti-Roman climate. It is beyond the scope of this work to delineate any further the specific anti-papal movements and activities in the different European countries of the day. In general, it can be stated that the papacy of the eighteenth century had been so battered by the ideologists on the one hand and by the absolute rulers and high ecclesiastics on the other hand, that in the minds of these men at least, the papacy had finally been reduced to its proper position -- the position, that is, of a mere Italian bishopric.[96]

Since St. Alphonsus lived in the immediate climate of the Bourbon Kingdom of Naples, it will be necessary to see, in summary form at least, just what the anti-papal climate was in this country. For the attitude of the rulers towards the Pope and the Holy See would, of course, greatly influence what he wrote in the defense of papal power.

The Kingdom of Naples had been ruled by Spanish kings and their viceroys since the early 1500's. Then, during the War of the Spanish Succession (1700-1713), the Archduke Charles of Austria succeeded in ascending the throne of Naples. This Austrian regime did not last long, however, for during the War of the Polish Succession, the Bourbon King, Philip V of Spain (1733-1738) reconquered Naples and made it into an independent country, ruled by his son Don Carlos. In the year 1759, Don Carlos' elder brother, Ferdinand VI of Spain died, and Don Carlos became King of Spain, as Charles III. In taking over the throne of Spain, Charles III left Naples to his third son, Ferdinand IV who was only eight years old. Hence, Charles continued to rule Naples from Spain through his Neapolitan prime minister, Bernardo Tanucci. However, some years later, when Ferdinand married Marie-Caroline of Austria in 1767, he rid himself of his father's influence and took over the reins of government himself. Then in 1776 he dismissed Tanucci and put the Marquis della Sambucca in his place.[97]

Under the Bourbon dynasty especially, the regalist and Gallican theories of the time made great progress in the Kingdom of Naples. As a matter of fact, these theories found a more fruitful soil in Naples than in many another European country.[98] So greatly were they put into effect that Rinieri has stated that Ferdinand

31

IV made more inroads into the purely ecclesiastical territory of the Church of Naples than even Protestant England made in the English Church.[99]

There were several reasons why such antipapal theories would find willing ears in this Neopolitan Kingdom: 1) the Normans many years before had given the Kingdom of Naples in fief to the Holy See. Thus, the necessity of recognizing the kingdom's vassalage to the Pope bred an anti-papal mentality in the rulers of Naples for centuries.[100] 2) Naples was economically unstable in the eighteenth century. This was due, in part, to the clerical possession and control of a considerable portion of the land of the kingdom. All lands held by the Church were held in mortmain. Thus, to check the increase of mortmain and so to keep the control of the Church's properties under the hand of the government, the liberties of the Church were attacked again and again with the regalist and gallican principles. The final aim of such attacks was, of course, a complete usurpation of the authority of the Church and consequently of much of its temporal holdings.[101] 3) The Kingdom of Naples was overcrowded with priests and religious. Colletta, in his Storia del Reame di Napoli held that the proportion between the total population and the clergy was twenty-eight to one thousand.[102] According to De Meulemeester, this is an exaggeration, since Colletta was very biased against the Church. But that the proportion was high cannot be denied. In 1742, the Stato delle Anime of the Archbishop of Naples listed 4575 male and 3183 female religious for the city of Naples alone.[103] Such a large amount of priests and religious would, in the eyes of the rulers, constitute a real danger to the economically unstable condition of the kingdom. It could also give the Church in Naples too great influence.

Add these special conditions to the general tenor of the times, and it can be seen why political gallicanism or regalism would find a good climate in which to grow in the Kingdom of Naples. The name this political Gallicanism usually went by in Naples was jurisdictionalism, because it was the Italian jurists who developed and elaborated the principles on which it acted.[104] For the Gallicans and regalists in France, Germany, Spain, and the Low Countries had their counterparts in the jurists of the Kingdom of Naples. There was Nicholas Caravita who in 1707 published his <u>Nullum Jus Pontificis in Regnum Neapolitanum</u>. There was Gaetano Argento, who in his different dissertations on law endowed the king with a sacred personality with equal rights over both civil and ecclesiastical affairs. And there were Constantino Grimaldi and Alexander Riccardi who also defended the right of the king against the Holy See. Most important among all these jurists was Pietro Giannone who in his <u>Istoria Civile del Regno di Napoli</u> (1723) summed up into one organic whole the regalist and Gallican principles of the other jurists. This work, which was placed on the Index immediately, gave Tanucci and his successors a strong formula for the principles which they were to put into effect for the next fifty years.[105]

Don Carlos, or Charles III, the first Bourbon king of Naples, although a deeply religious man, was thoroughly imbued with the principles of jurisdictionalism. As a Bourbon he was greatly influenced by the gallican courts of Paris and Madrid. Hence, when he ascended the throne of Naples, the anti-papalism, or anti-curialism as it came to be known, which had been present under the Spanish and Austrian regimes took a definite upsurge. And when in 1755 he chose the jurist Bernardo Tanucci as his Chancellor of State, Naples became intensely anti-curial.[106]

As in the other countries of Europe, this anti-curialism came to be closely allied with the Jansenists. Thus Giannone, Grimaldi, Riccardi and many of the jurists were also Jansenists. The Jansenists of course allied themselves with the regalists because they found in them a common enemy against Rome. For Rome had condemned both the Jansenists and the regalist or gallican principles many times over![107] Thus, the two had a common cause. In 1758, an incident occurred which helped to weld their cause into a more united effort. In that year Rome condemned an Italian translation of Mesenguy's French catechism, because the work was Jansenistic. This translation had been approved, however, by the ministers of state in Naples. Such a condemnation by Rome of a state approved catechism was looked upon as a total disregard of Neapolitan liberties. The incriminations and accusations which followed Rome's act joined the Jansenists and Regalists in even closer contact in their struggle against Rome.[108]

However, Bernardo Tanucci, Charles III's Chancellor of State and Minister of Justice, was not a Jansenist. Though he might resent Rome's condemnation of a book which had met with state approval, still he himself had no patience with the inflexible and stern attitude of the Jansenists. Neither was he a free-thinker. He deeply hated the materialist and deist theories of the day which he called a metaphysics with no foundation. One would have to live in his environment to understand how a man could hate Roman authority as vehemently as Tanucci did, and hate any authority which Rome might try to exercise over the Church in Naples, and yet at the same time be a good living Catholic. Tanucci's actions were not, however, guided by any irreligious spirit. They were guided by an entirely erroneous concept of the relationship between Church and State. He did not think that he was destroying the Church when he fought against the authority of Rome. He was simply preventing a foreign power from invading the territory of the State. In his eyes, the king was the minister of God in the State. It was the king -- not a foreign sovereign -- who was the pastor of his people and the defender of Church and State. It was the duty of the king to provide not merely for the temporal well-being of his subjects, but also for their spiritual well-being. Hence, it was his duty to supervise the observance of the laws of the Church and to guard Christian doctrine and morals.[109]

Tanucci, who was once professor of Canon Law at the University of Pisa, had ample time and opportunity to study and develop for himself these theories of the relation between the Church and State.[110] Once Charles made him Chancellor of State, these theories had a place to be exercised. He exercised them so completely, and so pushed his regalist principles to their ultimate extreme, that even the regalist ministers of Spain considered many of his actions and his intolerant attitude as distasteful.[111]

Under Charles III, Tanucci's anti-curial actions were somewhat restricted. But once he took over the regency under Ferdinand IV, he could give such actions full sway. It was during this regency especially that Tanucci labored to establish a state Church. He restricted the jurisdiction of the Bishops, impeded any increase in the mortmain, and reduced the taxes that were to be paid to the Roman curia from the ecclesiastical properties. He established the principle that not more than ten priests should be ordained for every thousand souls, and later reduced this number to five. The King's placet or exequatur for all papal bulls was vigorously enforced. Censures by the Bishops which laymen incurred by obedience to the State laws were annulled. Tanucci insisted more and more upon the State's right of the nomination of Bishops. The Holy See on its side refused to let this right be abused. As a result, many of the bishoprics and abbeys fell vacant, and the revenues went to the State. He diminished the number of monasteries, and combined four bishoprics into one. Appeals to Rome were forbidden without the royal permission. Holy Matrimony was declared a civil contract, and all matrimonial cases were to be tried in civil courts. And in 1767, the Jesuits were expelled from the Kingdom of Naples. After Ferdinand IV married Marie-Caroline of Austria, the regency ended. But Tanucci continued as Chancellor of State and continued in his anti-curial policies. For Ferdinand was not greatly interested in the things of State. Finally, to shake off the influence of Spain, Marie-Caroline had Ferdinand dismiss Tanucci in 1776. He died seven years later in 1783.[112]

It was in such a climate that St. Alphonsus lived and wrote and founded his Congregation. These regalist or gallican theories of the day had become so much part of the thought of the Kingdom that even some of the priests of his own Congregation were infected with these ideas. Some of the members doubted the validity of their rule, because, although it had been approved by Rome, this approval had not received the royal placet or exequatur.[113] De Meulemeester states that this situation was not surprising since the State had monopolized education. The chairs of the universities were occupied by the teachers of anti-curialism, and their doctrine found its way into all branches of education. Thus the younger generation was very much affected by the atmosphere of hostility toward the supreme authority of the Church![114]

Many of the letters of St. Alphonsus speak of the regalist theories of the day. For example, he states in one: "Here in Naples, terrible decrees are issued against the poor Churches every day. 'Peace is near,' we always hear people say; but decrees fall thick as snowflakes."[115] In his first report to the Sacred Congregation of the Council of the state of his diocese, he informs the Congregation that he has not been able to hold a diocesan synod since, "because of the circumstances in which we are situated at present, the Bishops cannot enact and publish synodal statutes."[116] Many other of his letters talk of the great difficulties he had getting his Congregation approved by the State in such an anti-papal, anti-clerical atmosphere and of the constant interference in the internal governing of his Congregation by the ministers of State![117] Still others show the Neapolitan government interfering again and again in matters of doctrine![118] The difficulties which Alphonsus had in getting many of his own doctrinal works approved, especially those dealing with papal authority will be discussed in the next chapter of this work. He was finally so discouraged at all this interference that he wrote in 1772:

> This (The History of Heresies) will be my last work, as I do not intend to write any more on scientific subjects. I do not want to have anything more to do with censors who have so tormented me. Should I publish any more in the future, it will only

be on a devotional character ... Let what I have done suffice. I shall soon complete my seventy-seventh year, and it is time that I should begin to think only of death, which is upon me.[119]

From this brief summary of the anti-papal movements and theories of the day, it can be seen how much the Church needed champions of her God-given authority. St. Alphonsus de Liguori was one of these champions. His works in defense of papal authority carried on the work of such men as Cardinal Sfondrati,[120] the Jesuit, Becano,[121] the Capuchin Roverio,[122] D'Aguirre,[123] Rocaberti,[124] Petit-Didier,[125] Tirso Gonsalez,[126] Lupus,[127] Duval[128] and many others who, as Cacciatore says, were writers of no mediocre talent.[129]

NOTES TO CHAPTER I

1. S. Alphonso M. de Liguori, *Opere Ascetiche* volume 1 - (Rome, 1933 -)
2. S. Alphonsus, *Opera Moralia* in 4 vols. (Rome, 1905 -)
3. See chapter two of this work which gives the full list of St. Alphonsus' writings on papal power.
4. L. Sturzo, *Church and State* (London, 1939) ch. 1 and 2.
5. P. Hughes, *A History of the Church* 1 (New York, 1948) 187.
6. L. Sturzo, *Nationalism and Internationalism* (New York, 1946) 14.
7. L. Sturzo, *Church and State* 117, 254 et al.
8. L. Sturzo, *Nationalism and Internationalism* 14.
9. Ibid. 15.
10. C. Hayes, *History of Modern Europe* 1 (New York, 1939) 23 - 27.
11. E. Butler, "The Catholic Church and Modern European Civilization" in E. Eyre's *European Civilization, its Origins and Developments* 6 (Oxford, 1937), 1345ff.
12. C. Hayes, *op. cit.* 225.
13. Ibid. 189.
14. C. Goodwin, *Papal Conflict with Josephism* (New York, 1938) 40.
15. E. Preclin - E. Jarry, *Les Luttes Politiques et Doctrinales aux XVIIe et XVIIIe Siecles* in Fliche-Martin, *Histoire De L'Eglise* 19 (Paris, 1955) 66. Pereira's book was placed on the Index in 1642, but the condemnation was never published in Europe. Ibid.
16. C. Hayes, *op. cit.* 291.
17. Ibid.

18. M. Declareuil, Histoire General du Droit Francaise (Paris, 1925) 444.
19. J. Lecler, The Two Sovereignties (New York, 1952), 148.
20. M. Dubruel, "Gallicanisme" DTC 6/1 (1947) 1096 - 1137. See 1096 - 97.
M. Dubruel - H.X. Arquilliere, "Gallicanisme" DAFC 2 (1912) 193 - 274. See especially 193ff. Preclin-Jarry, op. cit. 149 - 150.
21. M. Dubruel, art. cit. 1107.
22. Dubruel-Arquilliere, art. cit.
23. A. Baudrillart, "Constance (Concile de)" DTC 3/1 (1938) 1197 - 1224. See 1203 - 1206, esp.
24. Mansi, 27, 585.
25. Mansi, 29, 53 and 56.
26. Mansi, 29, 59.
27. Mansi, 29, 78.
28. A. Baudrillart, "Bale (Concile de)" DTC 2/1 (1932), 113 - 129. See especially, 125 - 129.
C. Hefele, Histoire des Conciles 7/2 (Paris, 1916) 844n.
29. Thus, some Gallicans like Edmund Richer held that the whole Council was ecumenical and its decrees binding on all. Others, like Bossuet thought that it was ecumenical until 1437. Still others admitted the ecumenicity of the first sixteen sessions. Any one of these opinions give the Gallicans strong arguing points. "Bale", art. cit. 125.
30. L. Sturzo, Church and State, 160.
R. Aubenas, "Le Pontificat de Jules II et les debuts de Leon X" in Fliche-Martin, Histoire de L'Eglise 15 (Paris, 1951) 171ff.
31. R. Aubenas, art. cit. 175.
32. R. Aubenas, art. cit. 181.
33. Preclin-Jarry, op. cit. 153.
34. L. Sturzo, Church and State, 304.

35. Ibid. 151-152. See also CL I, 800-802.
36. CL I, 812.
37. L. Sturzo, Church and State, 304.
38. CL I, 831 - 832.
39. CL I, 833 - 834.
40. CL I, 827 - 829.
41. L. Sturzo, Church and State, 304.
42. CL I, 89 - 92.
43. CL I, 835c
44. CL I, 835d
45. L. Sturzo, Church and State, 305.
46. Ibid. 250, 269, 330. 372.
Preclin-Jarry, op. cit. 87.
47. Preclin-Jarry, op. cit. 336, 628, 680-702.
R. Telleria, S. Alfonso M. de Ligorio 2 (Madrid, 1951). 258 - 264.
L. Sturzo, Church and State, 336.
L. Pastor, History of the Popes 31 (Herder, St. Louis, 1940) 85ff. Pastor states in this place that the reason why the Jesuits had been banished from Venice was because they had been submissive to the Pope.
A. Berthe, Life of St. Alphonsus M. de Liguori 2 (Dublin, 1905) 209 - 231.
A. Tannoia, Vida ed Istituto del Ven. S. d. Dio, Alfonso M. de Liguori 3 (Naples, 1802) 126ff.
48. Dom N. Jamin, Pensees Theologiques Relatives aux Erreurs du Temps Seventh Ed. (Paris, 1792) 121, 124, 125.
49. Ibid. 170 - 171
50. Ibid. 188, 194, 197, 204, 210, 212 - 213.
51. Ibid. 216, 218 - 223.
52. Ibid. 225.
53. V. Martin, e.g. gives three basic elements to the build-up of Gallicanism: 1: The independence of the king in all temporal affairs; 2: The limitation of papal power by former

conciliar decrees and canons; 3: The supremacy of a general Council over a Pope.
V. Martin, Origines du Gallicanisme 1 (Paris, 1939)

54. B. Tierney, Foundations of the Conciliar Theory (Cambridge, 1955) 23 - 24.
55. CJC I, Dist. 40, c. 6.
56. H.X. Arquilliere, "L'appel au concile sous Philippe le Bel" Revue des Questions Historiques 45 (1911) 23 - 55. and by the same author: "L'origine des theories conciliares" Seances et Travaux de l'Academie des Sciences Morales et Politiques 175 (1911) 573 - 586.
B. Tierney, op. cit. 1 - 20.
J.N. Figgis, From Gerson to Grotius Second Ed. (Cambridge, 1916) 41 - 70.
W. Ullman, Origins of the Great Schism (London, 1948) 9 - 56.
V. Martin, "Comment s'est formee la doctrine de la Superiorite du concile sur le Pape." Revue des Sciences Religieuses 17 (1937) 121 - 143; 261 - 289; 404 - 427.

57. L. Sturzo, Church and State, 153.
58. BR(T) 15, 720ff.
See: J. Carreyre, "Jansenisme" DTC 8/1 (1947) 319 - 529.
See 330 especially.
The Augustinus was first published in Louvain in 1640.

59. J. Carreyre, art. cit. 451.
60. Ibid. 500.
61. Ibid. 500ff.
Preclin-Jarry, op. cit. 195.
A. Arnauld, "Lettre a une personne de condition" Feb. 24, 1664. Oeuvres Completes 19 (Paris, 1783) 311 - 334.
A. Arnauld, "Seconde lettre a un duc et Pair de France" July 10, 1665. Oeuvres Completes 19 (Paris, 1783) 335 - 560.

62. Oeuvres Completes 17, 64ff.
63. Ibid. 21, 18 - 46.
64. This was the Constitution Ad sacram Beati Petri sedem of Pope Alexander VII (1655 - 1667) in which the Pope stated that the five propositions which had previously been condemned were truly taken from Jansenius' book, and condemned in Jansenius' sense. MBR 6, 47b.
65. L. Pastor, op. cit. 31, 203.
66. Ibid. 200.
67. Briefly, the cas de conscience was this: A French Cure had asked the theologians of Paris if a confessor could absolve a person who condemned the five propositions, but refused to attribute them to Jansenius, and who also refused to believe in the sufficiency of attrition for the Sacrament of Penance. The Paris theologians answered in the affirmative, and the great controversy was begun. Preclin-Jarry, op. cit. 215.
68. H. F. D'Aguesseau, "Observations sur le bref du Fevrier 12, 1703" Oeuvres de M. le Chancelier d'Aguesseau 13 (Paris, 1759) 330.
69. E. Preclin, Les Jansenistes du XVIII Siecle et la Constitution Civile du Clerge (Paris, 1929) 2.
70. Ibid. 22.
71. Ibid. 1 - 4.
72. Preclin-Jarry, op. cit. 769 - 778.
C. Goodwin, op. cit. 40.
L. Pastor, op. cit. 36, 251.
T. Ortolon, "Febronianisme" DTC 5/2 (1939) 2115 - 2124.
L. Sturzo, Church and State 269, 325.
73. L. Pastor, op. cit. 36, 251.
Preclin-Jarry, op. cit. 771 - 772.
74. L. Pastor, op. cit. 253.
75. A Singular Book of the lawyer, Justin Febronius on the state of the Church and the

<u>Legitimate Power of the Roman Pontiff, Written for the Purpose of Reuniting all the Protestants to the Christian Religion.</u>

76. T. Ortolan, <u>art. cit.</u> 2117.
77. <u>Ibid.</u>
78. <u>Febronius, op. cit.</u> Editio altera (Bologna, 1765) 1, 5, p.26; 1, 6, p. 32; 1, 7, p. 39; 3, 9, p. 198.
79. <u>Ibid.</u> 2, 1, p. 89; 2, 4, p. 104; 2, 10, p. 139; 2, 11, p. 142.
80. <u>Ibid.</u> 5, 2, p. 277; 6, 1, p. 357; 6, 4, p. 382; 6, 10, p. 444; 6, 11, p. 451.
81. <u>Ibid.</u> 7, 1, p. 534.
82. <u>Ibid.</u> 4, 6, p. 337.
83. <u>Ibid.</u> 9, 1, p. 697; 9, 5, p. 712 & 718.
84. L. <u>Pastor, op. cit.</u> 36, 262.
85. Published in two volumes at Pesaro, 1767.
86. L. <u>Pastor, op. cit.</u> 36, 262. Preclin-Jarry, <u>op. cit.</u> 773.
87. <u>Ibid.</u> Pastor, 265. <u>Ibid.</u> Preclin-Jarry, 774. See also: T. Ortolan, <u>art. cit.</u> 2119.
88. <u>MBR</u> 3, 450 - 451.
89. <u>Preclin-Jarry, op. cit.</u> 774.
90. <u>Ibid.</u> 776.
91. <u>Ibid.</u> 777.
92. See Chapter Two of this work.
93. Letter 271 to Don Giulio Selvaggio (LL 5, 72).
94. This Synod of Pistoia was the logical outcome of the Gallican, Jansenist, and regalist theories. It sought a complete reform of the Church, and introduced into its acts many Jansenistic and anti-papal decrees. Its acts were condemned by Pope Pius VI in the Constitution, Auctorem Fidei, August 28, 1794. BRC 9, 398ff. J. Carreyre, "Pistoie (Synode de)" <u>DTC</u> 12/2 (1935) 2134 - 2230.

95. Preclin-Jarry, op. cit. 778.
96. L. Pastor, History of the Popes 39 (St. Louis, 1952) 110.
97. M. De Meulemeester, Outline History of the Redemptorists (Louvain, 1956), 9 - 10.
Cantu, Storia Universale 10 (Turin, 1889), 406.
P. Coletta, Storia del Reame di Napoli (Milan, 1861) 44.
M. Schipa, Il Regno di Napoli sotto i Boboni (Naples, 1900) 19 - 21.
B. Croce, Storia del Regno di Napoli (Bari, 1931) 31.
98. De Meulemeester, op. cit. 10.
G. Cacciatore, Saint Alfonso De Liguori e il Giansenismo (Florence, 1944) 177ff.
99. I. Rinieri, Della Rovina d'una Monarchia (Turin, 1901) 514. L. Pastor, op. cit. 39, 123.
100. I. Rinieri, op. cit. 3 - 5.
R. Baylon, Como Escribio Alfonso de Ligorio (Madrid, 1940) 159.
101. De Meulemeester, op. cit. 11
G. Ruggiero, Il Pensiero Politico Meridionale nei Secoli XVIII e XIX (Bari, 1946) 6 - 7.
102. P. Coletta, op. cit. 27.
103. De Meulemeester, op. cit. 16.
He cites B. Capasso, Sulla Circoscrizione Civile ed Ecclesiastica e sulla Popolazione della Citta di Napoli (Naples, 1882) 72, as his source for the Stato delle Anime.
De Meulemeester quotes Cardinal Spinelli's report of 1736 to the Holy See in which the Cardinal himself stated that the large number of ecclesiastics in the kingdom constituted a real and grave disorder.
De Meulemeester, op. cit. 16.
R. Baylon, op. cit. 152.
104. De Meulemeester, op. cit. 11.
Cacciatore, op. cit. 177ff.

105. Cacciatore, op. cit. 179 - 181.
De Meulemeester, op. cit. 11
F. Nicolini, Le Teorie Politiche di Pietro Giannone (Naples, 1915) 110.
A. Jemolo, Il Giansenismo in Italia prima della Rivoluzione (Bari, 1925) 383ff.
A. C. Jemolo, Stato e Chiesa negli Scritoori Italiani del Seicento e del Settecento (Turin, 1914) 57, 92.
    106. De Meulemeester, op. cit. 12.
Cacciatore, op. cit. 178 - 179.
R. Telleria, S. Alfonso M. de Ligorio 1 (Madrid, 1950) 33.
R. Baylon, op. cit. 153 - 155.
The term "anti-curial" comes from the opposition of the regalists and jurists to the Roman Curia.
    107. Cacciatore, op. cit. 177 - 196.
    108. Ibid. 186 - 187.
    109. B. Croce, Uomini e Cose della Vecchia Italia 2 (Bari, 1927) 47 - 50.
G. Coniglio, "Tanucci" Enciclopedia Cattolica 11 (1954) 1735 - 1736.
R. Telleria, op. cit. 1, vi; 2, 486 - 488.
A. Berthe, Life of St. Alphonsus M. de Liguori 2 (Dublin, 1905) 2, 10, 33, 194 - 195.
L. Pastor, op. cit. 39, 110ff.
From what has been said of Tanucci, it is understandable why St. Alphonsus praised Tanucci for his piety and even dedicated his Trionfo della Chiesa, ossia Istoria delle Eresie (Venice, 1772) to him.
R. Telleria, op. cit. 2, 486ff.
A. Berthe, op. cit. 1, 292 - 294.
    110. P. Bazzi, "Tanucci" Dizionario Ecclesiastico 3 (1958) 1726 - 1735.
    111. R. Baylon, op. cit. 155 - 157.
    112. Pastor, op. cit. 39, 110ff.
Baylon, op. cit. 173ff.

Berthe, op. cit. 1, 549 - 550; 2, 213 - 231.
 113. De Meulemeester, op cit. 81.
A. Tannoia, op. cit. 4, 14, p. 64.
 114. Caciatore, op. cit. 201ff.
 115. Letter 689 to Father Blasucci (LL 2, 427). Sept. 8, 1771.
 116. Letter 355 to Sacred Congregation of the Council (LL 5, 287). July 8, 1765.
 117. Letters, Index (LL 5, 437).
 118. Ibid.
 119. Letter 255 to Remondini May 31, 1772 (LL 5, 33).
 120. Gallia Vindicata (Mantua, 1710)
 121. Controversia Anglicana ... (Mainz, 1612).
 122. Demonstrationes...2 (Lyons, 1617).
 123. Auctoritas infallibilis et Summa Cathedrae S. Petri (Salamanca, 1683).
 124. De Romani Pontificis Auctoritate (Valencia, 1691 - 94).
 125. De Auctoritate et Infallibilitate Summi Pontificis in Migne, Theologiae Cursus Completa 4.
 126. De Infallibilitate Romani Pontificis (Rome, 1683).
 127. Divinum ac immobile S. Petri ... Privilegium (Opera Omnia, Venice 1724 - 29, vol. 8.)
 128. Libelli de ecclesiastica et publica Postestate (Paris, 1612) This work was written against Edmund Richer.
Libelli de Suprema Romani Pontificis in Ecclesia Potestate (Paris, 1614). This work was written against Vigor, a defender of Richer.
I owe the above list of works to G. Cacciatore, op. cit. 306.
 129. G. Cacciatore, op. cit. 306.

CHAPTER II

THE WRITINGS OF
SAINT ALPHONSUS ON PAPAL AUTHORITY

Such a history of anti-papalism, plus the events of Tanucci's career in his own country of Naples, were certainly enough to make Saint Alphonsus, great lover of the papacy that he was, fear greatly for the Church in his own country and in the whole of Europe. It was in such an atmosphere that the Saint wrote his works in defense of papal authority. In this sphere of activity, he was not merely a speculative theologian working calmly at his desk on some treatise that would be beneficial to the scholastic advance of the Church; he was also a priest worried about the salvation of souls, worried that the anti-papal ideas would become such a part of the people's life that Christ's Church would indeed be a lost thing in the Kingdom of Naples! He was preeminently an apologist fighting against a particular evil, in a particular age. It was not his aim nor his task to write a full-blown thesis on Ecclesiology. Rather, it was his aim to explain especially to the ordinary man, the concept of papal authority. He also sought to defend that concept ably and profoundly against all adversaries, no matter who they might be but in language that ordinary people could understand. Once we have the general anti-papal background of the times in mind, and then, the particular anti-papal background of Saint Alphonsus' own country of Naples, it is much easier to see the

Saint's great concern to defend papal authority. It is characteristic of Saint Alphonsus, that, while he knew that many of his writings would be ill accepted by the Court of Naples, and might even spell ruin to the Congregation that he was trying so hard to found, still he knew that above all else, the Roman Pontiff and his authority must be defended. For the sake of this defense, he would sacrifice every dream of his own; even his life, as he himself declares:

> "With regard to the Supreme Power of the Sovereign Pontiff, I am ready to lay down my life in defense of that doctrine. Take that away, and I assure you, the authority of the Church is at an end."[2]

Before we examine the teaching of Saint Alphonsus on papal authority, it would be well to list all his works on papal authority and see some of the circumstances which inspired the individual works.

The first two dogmatic works which the Saint wrote were on the subject of the Pope and the Immaculate Conception - the two doctrines nearest to the heart of Saint Alphonsus - and the two doctrines, also, that were being so greatly attacked in his day.[3] His work on the Pope was called:

> Dissertatio de Romani Pontificis Auctoritate super Propositionem 29 damnatam ab Alexandro VIII, quae Dicebat: "Futilis et toties convulsa est assertio de Pontificis Romani supra concilium oecumenicum auctoritate atque in fidei quaestionibus decernendis infallibilitate.[4]

The work,

A Dissertation on the Authority of the Roman Pontiff in the light of the Twenty Ninth Proposition Condemned by Alexander VIII, which held: "The assertion that the Roman Pontiff has authority over an Ecumenical Council and has infallibility in defining questions of faith is futile and has been often disproved."

first appeared in 1748 in Saint Alphonsus' first edition of his Moral Theology, his Medulla Theologiae Moralis R.P. Hermann Busembaum, S.J., cum adnotationibus per R.P. Alphonsum de Ligorio, Rectorem Majorem Congregationis SS. Salvatoris, published in Naples by Pellechia. At first, the dissertation had no pagination and did not appear in the index of the work. This has led de Meulemeester to ask the question whether or not this work was first meant to be printed and sold separately.[5] Later, however, the work was considerably developed and made an integral part of the Moral Theology.[6]

The twenty-ninth condemned proposition mentioned in the title of this work was one of the thirty-one Jansenist propositions condemned by Alexander VIII in 1690. Even after the condemnation of the five propositions by Innocent X in his famous Constitution, Cum Occasione,[7] and the formulary prescribed by Alexander VII in 1665,[8] the Jansenists did not cease their activity, especially in the chairs of theology in Belgium. Consequently, in 1680, the Archbishop of Malines, and the other bishops of Belgium denounced these activities and errors to Rome. The Bishops' agent in preparing the memorial of condemnation was a certain Father Patrick Duffy, who was professor of theology in the University of Louvain. He prepared a list of ninety-six Jansenist errors, and from these,

Alexander VIII chose thirty-one which he considered the most dangerous and pernicious, and condemned them.[9]

Fifty-eight years later, when Saint Alphonsus came to write on papal authority, such a condemned proposition was an excellent point or departure for his work which would defend again these very two points which the Gallicans, Jansenists, and Regalists were still denying, i.e. the infallibility of the Pope in defining matters of faith, and his authority and superiority over a General Council. Because of this treatise, Saint Alphonsus had great difficulty in getting the Royal Censor to approve the work.[10] He wrote to his friend, the Basilian Abbot Muscari:

> "They (i.e. the Censors) have delayed the publication (of the Moral Theology) because of a dissertation which I had added as an end to the work on the power of the pope, in which I have shown how unsubstantial are the arguments of the French. Certainly, many have explained this matter, but I have summed up in an orderly and clear way the more essential things which are scattered throughout the authors. I have given this work no little study. It seems to me that it is a good work." [11]

Perhaps the answer to De Meulemeester's question as to whether or not this work was first meant to be published separately is answered here. Though we can find no record of his reasons (since it is evident that it would defeat his purpose if any letter or record were found), perhaps the Saint knew that the only way he could get his Dissertation approved was by including it in a work which he hoped would ultimately meet with the approval of the Royal Censors.[12]

The next work of Saint Alphonsus on papal authority was a work on forbidden books. It was called:

<u>Dissertatio de justa prohibitione et abolitione librorum nocuae lectionis brevi calamo plura continens quae diffuse ab auctoribus tradita sunt.</u>[13]

Father Berthe tells us:

"... the inundation of impious and immoral books which was flowing into Italy from France and Portugal had long excited anxiety in Alphonsus' breast."[14] "... since the state alone had the power to check the flood of evil literature... the Saint in his conversations with him about the importation of French books into the kingdom did not hesitate to point out to Cardinal Sersale, that an appeal to the King and his Ministers was the best weapon of defense..."[15]

In 1759, Saint Alphonsus decided to do something more drastic in order to combat the evil literature. (According to De Meulemeester, Saint Alphonsus determined to write this work only after making many useless supplications to both Brancone and Tanucci, begging them to stop such literature.[16]) We say "drastic", because to write such a work which the State would certainly consider subversive of its sovereign rights was indeed a dangerous step for the Saint to take. But the time had come for him to do something. It was bad enough that literature of such kind was coming into the State. But now, there were men who were defending the very reading of this literature. This the Saint could not tolerate. He himself gives us his reason for writing this

<u>Dissertation on the Just Prohibition and Destruction of Forbidden Books, Containing briefly many of the Doctrines which are Scattered among the Authors.</u>

He writes in the Preface to this work:

"Recently, I have come across two letters in which the very necessary and very salutary discipline of the Church on forbidden books has been attacked. It has been boldly asserted that one is allowed to read any book, as long as there is no evident danger of perversion in the book. This is directly against the law of the Church. The authors of these letters base their reasoning on two false principles:
First: that the law on forbidden books is of modern origin, and not found in the ancient law of the Church; and
Second: that the Church has not proceeded in a canonical way in this whole matter, nor observed the right order of law. Therefore, the law itself has no force ...
Since experience teaches that such depraved opinions destroy the authority of the Church and draw the faithful away from the proper obedience they owe to the definitions of the Church, and since, because of such opinions, the faithful fall into other errors against faith and morals to the immense shipwreck of their souls, I have written this dissertation to counteract such teachings..."[17]

This work was first published separately, as a small pamphlet. But in 1760, Saint Alphonsus instructed Remondini, his publisher, to include the work in his Moral Theology. It was, therefore, included in the fourth edition of the Moral, and has been in every edition since then.[18]

It is not to be expected that such a work would be easily passed by the royal censor. The Saint first had difficulty getting it approved for publication, and then more difficulty after it was published. About getting it passed, he wrote to Canon Sparano at Naples:

> "...About the book, we have arranged everything. It will be necessary for me to have certain pages reprinted; but we must have patience. Enough! I did not wish to yield at all, as the revisor wished me to do, and I did not insert a word that could redound to the injury of the Church."[19]

The work was finally passed by the royal censor, and then the storm broke out. Tanucci, who up to then had been ignorant of the existence of the Dissertation, when he did see it, sent his agents to destroy all copies on the spot, and threatened to disgrace the censor, Sacco, and to send the printer, Joseph di Domenico, to the galleys. Saint Alphonsus immediately wrote a letter to Tanucci, explaining that he did not intend to deny the rights of the King, but only to protect souls and ward off the ruin of the State. Tanucci actually changed his mind at the reception of this letter, and allowed the Dissertation to be circulated, but he never gave the reasons why he had such a change of mind.[20]

Saint Alphonsus' next complete work on papal authority (which is still extant[21]) was his book against Febronius. He called it:

<u>Vindiciae pro Suprema Romani Pontificis Potestate adversus Justinum Febronium, opella ab Honorio de Honoriis elucubrata.</u>[22]

This work,

<u>A Defense of the Supreme Power of the Roman Pontiff against Justin Febronius, a little work written by Honorius de Honoriis</u>

was published in 1768, and for very obvious reasons, under a psuedonym.

It will be noticed that there was a five year period between the publication of the <u>Febronius</u> and Saint Alphonsus' refutation of it. The reason for this was that only in 1767 had an Italian edition of the <u>Febronius</u> been put out and thus really threatened the thought of Saint Alphonsus' compatriots. This Italian edition, as has been noted above in Chapter I,[23] was published in Venice and received a thirty year privilege from the court at Venice. Such a work, summing up as it did all the anti-papal thought and principles of the day, needed a clear and concise answer, so that the ordinary people might have a ready answer to the false claims of the <u>Febronius</u>. Saint Alphonsus himself gives us the reason for writing his <u>Vindiciae</u>. In a letter to his publisher, Remondini, he says:

> "...I am engaged on the volume against F. (sic, standing for Febronius). I pray you in your letters to designate that author in this manner.
> I have put aside every other work in order to occupy myself solely with this little work. It is proving quite a taske for me... I was obliged to read two large tomes sent

to me from outside the Kingdom, and I am now waiting for another voluminous publication from Naples.

The book will not require more than ten or twelve folios, but I have to weigh every word carefully, as the work, being brief and written in Latin, will be perused by all, and by F. (sic) himself. I have seen published against F. many bulky tomes,[24] which will rarely be purchased and rarely read. Why? Because they are so voluminous and cost so much."[25]

Saint Alphonsus' work was relatively short considering that he had to write a complete answer to the main points of the Febronius which was a book of 650 pages. The Saint's work contained only 161 pages.

The difficulties which Saint Alphonsus faced in getting this work published were indeed great. It has already been noted[26] that the Febronius was greatly acclaimed by the regalists of the day. It became one of their chief weapons against the power of the Holy See. Ferdinand IV and Tanucci, with the other regalists of Naples, would not take it well that one of their own subjects had dared to write against such a work. This is the reason why Saint Alphonsus was afraid to mention even the name of his work in any of his letters. In a letter to Remondini, when he first mentioned the idea of writing such a work against Febronius, he says:

"Should you consent to the printing of this latter volume, I shall willingly recommence the task, even should the printing have to be done at my own expense..."[27] I must ... publish the pamphlet under an assumed name."[28]

Then, in a letter of May 20 to his publisher, the Saint speaks about how Remondini will receive the manuscript. The letter shows how extremely cautious one had to be in such matters:

> "...I have almost completed the work (you know to which one I allude) and in a short time you will receive, through Signor Moschini, the small box containing the manuscript. I must forwarn you that, for very good reasons, you will not find in it any letter from me, but instead a letter, or rather, a slip of paper with no signature. Do not try to divine the sense of the contents, as it is a letter without any meaning whatsoever. Be not surprised, therefore, if you cannot understand it..." [29]

On May 28, he sent to Remondini, under separate cover, the title-page of the work, and instructed him:

> "...For good reasons...I send you in the present letter, the title-page of the work. The manuscript that you will receive will contain no frontispiece..." [30]

In June of 1768, he changed his mind about sending the manuscript to Remondini, and had his printer in Naples secretly print a few copies for him. He writes to Remondini:

> "...a very strong reason which impelled me to have the work printed secretly here at Naples before forwarding it to you, is the great severity with which they treat such works in this capital. They need only open the little box and examine the manuscript, and I should see destroyed in an instant the

labor of eight months... This fear of losing the manuscript has been the chief motive that induced me to have the work printed at Naples... After that, I shall send you a copy. If it be lost, it matters little. I shall despatch another... I am thinking of sending you the sheets one by one in letters, just as they come from the press, as in that way, they will be more apt to reach you safely.

"This last plan will put me to some expense, but what does that matter? There is a question of defending the Church in the terrible trial through which she is passing.

"Another remark: if you could conceal your own name when you have the book printed, I should be very pleased..."[31]

And finally, in August of 1768, he wrote:

"...I have more than once spoken to you of my Dissertation on the spirituality of the soul (sic; in this way did the Saint refer to his Vindiciae), but I have not yet despatched it to you. I am waiting until I can find a secure way of sending it. My opponent is very intimate with the postal authorities, and I am afraid they may open my letters and the manuscripts confided to the courier. I cannot explain to you in detail how far his animosity extends..."[32]

At last, however, the Saint was able to get his work to Remondini and have it printed. Father Tellereia in his life of Saint Alphonsus, has this to say of the Vindiciae:

"It (the Vindiciae) is equivalent to proposing and solving the postulates of the Vatican Council a full century in advance.

Although in his own lifetime, these pages of Saint Alphonsus were not widely circulated, yet in the plans of Divine Providence, they were to have a great circulation in the following century..."[33]

The five works that have been mentioned are all the individual works which Saint Alphonsus wrote on papal authority. But as an integral part of both his Moral Theology and some of his dogmatic works, the Saint included several questions and treatises on the Pope and papal authority.

Scattered throughout his Moral Theology are questions on the Pope which indicate quite clearly the power which Saint Alphonsus considered vested in the Supreme Pontiff. He treats the following questions:

1: Whether the Pope can dispense one from solemn vows.[34]

2: Whether the Pope can commute last wills.[35]

3: Whether the Pope would sin gravely if he dispensed from the law of fasting without a reason.[36]

4: Whether the Pope is able to dispense so that one would be allowed to consecrate just one Species.[37]

5: Whether the Pope is able to dispense one from the law of repeating the marriage consent if the marriage is revalidated.[38]

6: Whether the Pope can dispense from a sacramental marriage.[39]

7: Whether the Pope can dispense one from solemn vows in order to marry.[40]

8: What are the impediments from which the Pope is able to dispense?[41]

9: Whether the Pope can dispense from those impediments which are of Divine Law.[42]

10: Whether the Pope is able to dispense from those impediments which are of the Natural law.[43]

In Saint Alphonsus' Dogmatic works there are more extensive treatises on the different aspects of papal authority. In 1762, he published a work in Italian called:

<u>Evidenza della Fede ossia Verita della Fede, fatta Evidente per li Contrassegni della sua credibilita.</u>[44]

In chapter IV of this short work,

<u>On the Evidence or Truth of the Faith which the Signs of Credibility make evident</u>

Saint Alphonsus speaks of the stability of the faith as a sign of credibility. He then goes on to prove the necessity of an infallible judge, who is the Roman Pontiff, in order that our faith remain stable. Christ Himself, the Saint goes on to say, established the Pope as this infallible judge and His Vicar on earth.[45]

This little work was a corollary to a previous work by the Saint against the materialists and Deists of the time, published in 1756.[46] He Called it:

> Breve Dissertazione contra gli errori de moderni Increduli, oggidi nominati materialisti e deisti.[47]

In this work,

> A Brief Dissertation against the errors of the modern Unbelievers, today called materialists and Deists

the Saint established the existence of a personal God, the immortality of the soul, and the fact of Divine Revelation. Then in his Evidenza Della Fede, he went on to prove that, among all religions, the Catholic Religion is the only true Religion, and the Catholic Faith the only true Faith.[48]

In 1767, Saint Alphonsus published a development of the two works just mentioned in a work called:

> Verita della Fede contro i materialisti che Negano l'esistenza di Dio, i Deisti che negano la Religione rivelata, ed i Settari che negano la Chiesa cattolica essere l'unica vera.[49]

In Part Three of this work,

> The Truth of the Faith against the Materialists Who deny the existence of God, against the Deists Who deny the fact of a revealed Religion, and Against the Protestants who deny that the Catholic Church is the one true Church.

there are three full chapters on the papacy.[50] In Chapter VIII, he proves that the Roman Pontiffs are the successors of Saint Peter, endowed with the very same power that Saint Peter had.[51] In Chapter IX, he proves the superiority of the Pope over a General Council.[52] And finally, in Chapter X, he proves that the Pope is infallible in defining questions of faith and morals.[53]

In one of his letters to Remondini, Saint Alphonsus gives us his motive for publishing this work. He says:

> "At present, I am writing a work against the modern heresies of atheists and Deists, since these errors are now everywhere in circulation. The Calvinists of England and the Jansenists of France are no longer Jansenists and Calvinists, but atheists and deists. They are continually scattering abroad books infested with their teaching. In Naples these books are sought after, and read, even by women, thus doing immense harm to souls." [54]

And again:

> "...works of the kind I am now engaged upon, require much clearness. I have read many treating of this subject, all of which, however, were most obscure. But having shown the first sheets of my volume to several persons, they assure me that they are most clear. I am, therefore, anxious to compose this work that, by irrefutable arguments, I may disabuse the unhappy victims of their errors." [55]

Surprisingly enough, even with the three full chapters on papal authority, this work had great success, so that the Saint himself could write:

"Thanks be to God, my book has met great success, and has had an extensive sale here, a rare event in Naples."[56]

In 1769, Saint Alphonsus published a work called:

<u>Opera Dommatica Contra Gli Eretici Pretesi Riformati</u>.[57]

This work,

<u>A Dogmatic Work against the heretical Psuedoreformers</u>,

was written, as Saint Alphonsus states in the Preface:

"...to explain the articles of Faith which the Council of Trent examined and defined; to expose the errors of the Reformers; and to give an answer to the difficulties raised against these very articles of Faith by Peter Suavis who excoriated the Council..."[58]

Peter Suavis who is mentioned in this preface was a psuedonym for Fra Paolo Sarpi,[59] a Venetian, who among his other deeds against the Church, and especially against the papacy, wrote: <u>I Storia del Concilio Trentino</u>.[60]

In a letter to Father Stephen Longobardi of Naples, Saint Alphonsus speaks about the work against the Reformers, and explains his reasons for writing it:

"I am this moment printing a very useful book, an abridgement of the History of the Council of Trent, by Cardinal Pallavicini,[61] which latter is very much confused.

"I know that Father Morelli...has already published a compendium of the work. It, also is confused. Pallavicini and Morelli speak of all the events, even political, that happened during the time of the Council. I limit myself to the dogmatic points of Faith defined by the Council...My work contains, therefore, sound dogma...I have placed at the end of the volume a very useful treatise on the infallibility of the Church, on the Rule of Faith, and on the necessity of an infallible judge..⁶²"

In this letter, the Saint gives us also his ultimate reason for all his writing. He says:

"My habitual infirmities confine me to bed, but I am free from fever, and my head is still strong. I have, consequently, more time at my disposal to compose one or the other book for the glory of God and the good of the Church. Little do they print nowadays in defence of the Church in comparison with all they publish for her destruction.⁶³."

Of interest here in this study of Saint Alphonsus' teaching on papal authority, is the treatise at the end of this work on the infallibility of the Church, the Rule of Faith, and the necessity of an infallible judge, which he speaks of in his letter.⁶⁴ He called this treatise:

<u>Della Ubidienza dovuta alle definizioni del concilio E per conseguenza della Chiesa cattolica Romana, fuori di cui non vi e salute.</u>⁶⁵

Or:

On the Obedience due to the Definitions of a Council, and in consequence to the Roman Catholic Church, outside which there is no salvation.

In 1772, Saint Alphonsus published his longest work in the field of Dogmatic Theology, his:

Trionfo della Chiesa ossia Istoria delle Eresie Colle lore Confutazioni.[66]

Saint Alphonsus got the idea of writing this

Triumph of the Church, or a History of Heresies And Their Confutation,

after finishing his work against the Protestant Reformers. In studying all the heresies of the Protestants, he found that they were but an echo of the ancient heresies in the Church. So he decided to give a history of all the major heresies and show how the Church has successfully handled each heresy and risen victorious above each one.[67]

In this work, too, Saint Alphonsus treated some aspects of papal authority. In dealing with the Monothelite heresy, he explains the position of Pope Honorius and argues that the Pope did not fall into heresy.[68] Then in the second part of the work, the Saint confutes all the heresies which have been mentioned in the first part. In his eleventh confutation where he treats the errors of Luther and Calvin, he speaks on the infallible power of the Church, and the authority of a General Council. While treating these two points, he shows the relationship of the pope to the infallible power of the Church, and to a General Council.[69]

One of the last works of the Saint was:

> Dissertazione Theologiche-morali appartenenti alla vita eterna.[70]

This work,

> A Theological-Moral Dissertation on Those Things Which pertain to Eternal Life,

was published by the Saint in 1776, just eleven years before he died. He had planned a great work, indeed, a full Eschatology,[71] but his health failed him, and he was able to complete only a part of the work.[72] In this work, Saint Alphonsus gives a list of the signs of the end of the world. One of the signs, the second sign, will be a defection of faith and a defection from the obedience due to the Sovereign Pontiff.[73]

Thus even to the very end of his life, Saint Alphonsus' writings turned again and again to a defense of the authority of the Pope. It was truly a central doctrine in his life. Seeing these many writings of the Saint on papal authority, it is not hard to understand why the popes, down through the years, have singled out and praised his defense of papal power.

Gregory XVI in his Bull of Canonization of St. Alphonsus, says:

> "Alphonsus Maria Liguori was wonderfully skilled, especially in sacred doctrine...He wrote many books, to guard the morals of the people; to defend the truth of the Catholic Religion; to assert the rights of this Holy Apostolic See..."[74]

In a decree of the Sacred Congregation of

Rites, approved by Pius IX, in which the title of <u>Doctor Ecclesiae</u> was conferred on Saint Alphonsus, we read:

> "Certainly, St. Alphonsus M. de Liguori is worthy to be numbered among those who worked and taught, and whom Christ would call great in the Kingdom of Heaven. He dispelled and removed the darkness of errors spread so widely by the unbelievers and the Jansenists...He made clear what was obscure, and settled questions in doubt ...He clearly illustrated and boldly asserted the doctrines of the Immaculate Conception and the infallibility of the Roman Pontiff when he speaks <u>ex cathedra</u>...[75]"

Pope Pius IX in the Apostolic Letter in which he made Saint Alphonsus a Doctor of the Church says:

> "When the doctrine of the Jansenists... was attracting many with its form of error and confusing many, God in His marvellous Providence most powerfully raised up Alphonsus M. de Liguori...who...would open his mouth in the midst of the Church and by his learned and laborious writings would see to it that this pestilence that had risen from the depths of hell would be torn up by its roots. He wrote many books...to give directors of souls a safe path in which to guide the souls under their care; to inform and instruct the clergy; to confirm and defend the truth of the Catholic Faith against heretics of any kind or name; and to assert the rights of the Apostolic See.[76]"

And finally, in a letter to Fathers Dujardin and

and Jacques, Pope Leo XIII wrote:

"...he (Saint Alphonsus) guarded Divine Revelation with solid arguments against the Deists; he strongly defended the truth of our Faith; he most efficaciously asserted the Immaculate Conception of the Mother of God; he boldly proposed the primacy and the infallible teaching power of the Roman Pontiff...[77]"

It now remains to study the contents of these writings of St. Alphonsus and to see his full teaching on the concept of papal authority.

NOTES TO CHAPTER II

1. G. Cacciatore, "Alfonso Maria de' Liguori," EC 1 (1948) 866
B. Haering, E. Zettl, "Alfons Maria de Liguori", LTK 1 (1957) 330

2. Letter 251 to Don Giulio Selvaggio, Feb. 22, 1772 (LL 4. 19)

3. R. Tellereia, San Alfonso Maria de Ligorio (Madrid 1951) 1. 421

4. St. Alphonsus, Theologia Moralis, Lib. 1, Dub. 2, Cap 1, n. 110 - 135 (OMG 1, 93 - 121)

5. De Meulemeester, Bibliographie Generale des Ecrivains Redemptoristes (Louvain, 1933) 1. 65 n 2.

6. Ibid

7. Cum Occasione, May 31, 1653 (MBR 5, 486 b, Denziger, 1092 ff)

8. Regiminis Apostolici, Feb. 15, 1665 (MBR 6 212 a, Denz. 1099)

9. X. Le Bachelet, "Alexandre VIII," DTC 1 (1930) 751

10. In the Kingdom of Naples at the time of Saint Alphonsus, there were two censors, the Royal Censor who was appointed directly by the King, and the Ecclesiastical Censor.

11. This letter is quoted by Tellereia, op. cit. 1, 422. He does not give the original, but only his own Spanish translation. The original is published in the periodical, Sant Alfonso, 12 (1941) 199. The author of the present work was not able to obtain this periodical.

12. In the third edition of Saint Alphonsus' Theologia Moralis (1757), there is a "Dissertatio Prologemena" by Anthony Zacharia, S.J. In this "Dissertatio", there is a section called "De Romanorum Pontificium Decretis Eorumque

usu in Morali Theologia." Jule Jacques in his work Du Pape et du Concile (Tournai, 1869), 691 gives the impression that this work is by St. Alphonsus himself. Monsignor Lupoli in his edition of the Omnia Opera of Saint Alphonsus gives the same wrong impression. (Liguori, Opere (Venezia 1840) 1. 5.)

    13. Theologia Moralis, Lib. I, Tract. II, App III (OMG I) 253 - 291.

    14. A. Berthe, Life of St. Alphonsus de Liguori, tr. from French by H. Castle (1905 Dublin) 1. 552

    15. Ibid, 508

    16. M. De Meulemeester, op. cit. 1. 103 - 104

    17. Dissertatio de justa ...(OMG I, 253).

    18. M. De Meulemeester, op. cit. 1. 104.

    19. Letter 325 to Canon Sparano, Sept. 7, 1759 (LL 1. 541).

    20. A. Berthe, op. cit. 1. 554 - 555.

    21. Two of the Saint's works on papal authority have been lost. One was called: Riflessi spettanti alla dichiarazione dell'Assemblea di Franca circa l'infallibilita del papa. According to Father Tannoia in his Vida, this work was published in Naples, 1765. On the authority of Father Tannoia, both C. Villecourt and the Editors of the Actus Doctoratus list this book as among the works of Saint Alphonsus, but then go on to state that it has been lost.

    A. Tannoia, Vida ed Instituto de S.A. d. L. (Naples, 1798-1802) 3. c. 7.

    C. Villecourt, Vie Institut de Saint Alphonse M. d. L. (Tournai, 1868) 4. 343

    Concessionis Tituli Doctoris in honorem S. Alphonsi M. de Liguori (Rome, 1870) 1. 13. The other lost work was called: Dissertatio de Romani Pontificis Auctoritate (1777?) Father J. Jacques thinks that this work and the Riflessi mentioned above are one and the same work. But Father M. De Meulemeester does not agree with him. He thinks that this work of 1777 was a new work, but in his opinion, it was never published.

J. Jacques, op. cit. xxxiv

M. De Meulemeester, op. cit. 1. 130, 179, 190.

22. ODW I, 383 - 459. In French: J. Jacques, op. cit. 187 - 396.

23. Vide supra, cap I.

24. E.g. Father Anthony Zacharia had written a work against Febronius which was in five volumes: Anti-febronio...(Pesaro, 1767).

25. Letter 203 to Remondini, April 28, 1768 (LL 4. 392).

26. Vide supra, cap. I.

27. Here is a good example of Saint Alphonsus' great love of the papacy. He refused in general to make any money on any of his works, but for such an important book, he would be willing to lose money.

28. Letter 197 to Remondini, Feb. 18, 1768 (LL 4. 381).

29. Letter 204 to the same, May 20, 1768 (LL 4. 394).

30. Letter 205 to the same, May 28, 1768 (LL 4. 396).

31. Letter 207 to Remondini, June 1768 (LL 4. 401)

32. Letter 213 to the same, August 3, 1768 (LL 4. 411)

33. Tellereia, op. cit. 2, 338.

34. An Papa queat dispensare in votis solemnibus
Theologia Moralis, 3. 256 (OMG I) 538.

35. An commutare ultimas voluntates.
Theol. Mor., 3, 931 (OMG II) 334.

36. An Papa peccet graviter, si dispenset

in jejunio sine causa.
Theol. Mor.,3. 1032 (OMG II) 416.

37. An possit dispensare ad consecrandum unam tantum speciem.
Theol. Mor., 6, 196, dub 2 (OMG III) 176.

38. An in novo consensu, si matrimonium sit revalidandum.
Theol. Mor. 6, 897, Prob. 1 in fine (OMG IV) 76.

39. An in Matrimonio rato.
Theol. Mor. 6, 959 (OMG IV) 139.

40. An in solemni voto ad ineundem matrimonium.
Theol. Mor. 6, 1026 (OMG IV) 181.

41. In quibus impedimentis possit dispensare.
Theol. Mor. 6, 1118 (OMG IV) 247.

42. An in illis quae sunt de jure divino.
Theol. Mor. 6, 1119 (OMG IV) 248.

43. An quae sunt de jure naturae.
Theol. Mor. 6, 1120 (OMG IV) 249.

44. ODN 8, 1 - 45; ODW 1, 43 - 84.
45. ODN 8, 19 - 20; ODW 1, 61.
46. De Meulemeester, op. cit. 1, 86
47. Evidenza, ODN 8, 1 - 30; ODW 1, 5 - 31.
48. Evidenza, ODN 8, 4; ODW 1, 7.
49. ODN 8. 1 - 245; ODW 1. 99 - 378.
50. ODN 8. 174 - 222; ODW 1. 300 - 360.
51. ODN 8. 174 - 177; ODW 1. 300 - 303.
52. ODN 8. 177 - 210; ODW 1. 303 - 344.
53. ODN 8. 210 - 222; ODW 1. 344 - 360.
54. Letter 167 to Remondini, Dec. 19, 1765 (LL 4. 333).
55. Letter to Remondini, Feb. 5, 1766 (LL4. 340)
56. Letter 191 to the same, July 21, 1767 (LL 4. 372)
57. ODN 8. 1 - 211; ODW 1. 465 - 717.

58. ODN 8. 1; ODW 1. 465.
59. E. Amann, "Sarpi" <u>DTC</u> 14 (1939) 1115 - 1121
60. Pietro Soave Polano, I storia del Concilio Tridentino...<u>A History of the Council of Trent</u> (London 1619).
61. The abridgement the Saint speaks of here is his <u>Opera Dommatica Contra Gli Eretici</u>...
62. Letter 218 to Father Longobardi, March 13, 1769 (LL 4. 422).
63. Ibid.
64. vide supra.
65. ODN 8. 197 - 207; ODW 1. 703 - 717.
66. ODN 8. 1 - 425; ODW 2. 1 - 503.
67. <u>Trionfo</u>...(ODN 8) 5; (ODW 2) 7.
68. <u>Trionfo</u>...I, VII, a. 2, n. 7 - 10 (ODN 8) 111 - 112; (ODW 2) 139 - 140.
69. <u>Trionfo</u>...II, Confutazione XI, # 7 (ODN 8) 358; (ODW 2) 440.
<u>Trionfo</u>...II, XI # 8 (ODN 8) 359 - 366; (ODW 2) 441 - 449.
70. ODN 8. 1 - 76; ODW 2. 535 - 627.
71. Letter 302 to Remondini, Aug. 28, 1776 (LL 5. 119).
72. Letter 305 to the same, Nov. 15, 1776 (LL 5. 123).
73. Dissertazione theologiche...4 # 2 (ODN 8) 16; (ODW 2) 554.
74. <u>Acta Gregorii PP. XVI</u>, II (ed. Bernasconi, Rome 1901) 394.
75. Concessionis tituli Doctoris in honorem S. Alphonsi de Ligorio, Decretum Urbis et Orbis, <u>Acta Sanctae Sedis</u>, VI, (1870) 318.
76. Litterae apostolicae de S. Alfonso M. de Ligorio titulo Ecclesiae Doctoris aucto, Pius PP. IX, <u>ASS</u>, VI (1870) 320.

77. Letter to Fathers Dujardin and Jacques, C.SS.R., Pope Leo XIII, (August 23, 1879) quoted by J. Jansen, Testimonia de S. Alfonso de Ligorio (1928) 27.

CHAPTER III

SAINT ALPHONSUS' CONCEPT OF PAPAL AUTHORITY

Before studying the arguments which Saint Alphonsus used to establish papal authority, it is important to know his basic concept of supreme power in the Pope. Ever since the battle over papal infallibility before its definition at the Vatican Council, the concept of papal authority has been greatly obfuscated, at least in the popular mind. For during the battle that raged prior to the definition of papal infallibility, the impression was given that the whole essence of papal power lay in papal infallibility. This, of course, is not true. While men fought greatly either for or against papal infallibility, the third chapter of the dogmatic constitution De Ecclesia Christi in which the Fathers of the Council defined the basic concept of papal authority, was passed over almost in silence! Yet this was the definition men should have fought about. For once the essence of papal authority was defined in the terms used by the Council, then the charism of infallibility had to be predicated of the Pope. It followed as an effect flows naturally from its cause. As Corrigan puts it:

> "The dogma of papal infallibility is in the minds of many, the sole achievement of the Vatican Council. It loomed so large in the acrid discussions before, during, and after the Council, inside and outside the

Vatican; it carried so much of intrinsic human interest; its genesis can be traced in such detailed and voluminous records; its consequences have been considered so awful; it was so timed in its final adoption, that historians and writers...have been prone to see nothing else. But the doctrine is contained in a single chapter of the two condensed 'Constitutions' of the Council. It is...but the crowning conclusion of the Constitution on papal primacy. It exalts the supreme teaching office of the Pope, and throws around it, in certain restricted circumstances, the charism of inerrancy for the greater security of all believers."[2]

In the mind of Saint Alphonsus, this relationship between papal power and papal infallibility was most clear. For him, in the essence of papal authority lay all the privileges and power of the Pope. When men attacked this or that power of the Pope, Saint Alphonsus did, indeed, defend the particular power attacked; but he always came back to the very essence of papal authority. He first established what this papal authority really was, and having once established this, it was easy to refute the arguments against some particular papal power.

His reason for the necessity of a Supreme Ruler in the Church is concisely stated:

"After Christ, the Lord finished the work of our redemption, He promised the Church His assistance and that of the Holy Spirit until the end of time. He said:

'And behold, I am with you all days, even till the consummation of the world.' and:

'But when He, the Spirit of truth has come, He will teach you all truth.'[3]

"Now since Our Redeemer, the principle founder of the Church, the head and pastor, was going to leave this world, it was necessary that He leave some visible head and supreme judge in the Church, who taking His place, would define by an infallible judgement things of faith and morals, so that the unity of faith might be preserved forever, and so that the faithful might not be always in a state of doubt at the lack of a legitimate authority who could stop a controversy by an absolutely certain definition which all would be bound to obey. Such a head was necessary lest schisms and contentions disturb the Christian world..."[4]

Once he has stated the reason for a Supreme Ruler, the Saint goes on to define the power that lies vested in such a Ruler:

"We maintain that the primacy of the Roman Pontiff is not one of direction only, consisting in simple vigilance, exhortations, admonitions, and dependent upon the consent of the Church. We maintain that it is a true primacy of power and jurisdiction."[5]

"(This) primacy of jurisdiction was given to Peter that from this one source, power might be communicated to the other ministers of the Church, and thus, there might be one Church, and one Cathedra."[6]

"Inseparably flowing from (this primacy of power and jurisdiction) by divine institution are these following rights:

1: To pronounce judgement on those cases which are called 'major'.

2: To enforce laws which oblige the universal Church, as long as they have been sufficiently promulgated.

3: To receive appeals from the whole Christian world, even in the first instance.

4: To have authority over the General Councils, and ordinary power over all the faithful." [7]

And in his <u>Moral Theology</u>, the Saint adds this right:

5: "With a just cause, to dispense from some things which are of divine right and concern human acts" (the Saint gives the case of a <u>ratum non-consummatum marriage</u>). [8]

Saint Alphonsus shows, however, that this supreme power of the Pope does not extend over the whole of man's life, and that the Pope as Vicar of Christ upon earth, is not the master of the earth, as is Christ. The Pope is Christ's Vicar for Christ's Church, and there are many things which do not fall under his jurisdiction. The Saint treats the question whether or not the Pope is able to dispense from wills, made for pious causes, without a sufficient reason. His answer:

"No...the Pope is not the master of such goods; he is, therefore, not able either from ordinary power, or from extraordinary power to change the dispositions of a will, without reason..."⁹

One of the major rights, of course, which flow from the Pope's true promacy of power and jurisdiction is his infallibility:

> "...he who would refute Febronius must prove him wrong in his sophistic opposition to the supreme authority of the Pope and his privilege of infallibility which necessarily follows from his supreme authority. For the Pope would not be supreme unless he were infallible.... Once we have established that the authority of the Pope in the Church is supreme and infallable, then all controversies cease and vanish."¹⁰

When does the Pope exercise this charism of personal infallibility? The Saint tells us:

> "Some authors teach that the Pope is infallible in defining things of faith and morals only when he
>
> 1: Proceeds maturely;
>
> 2: Has heard the judgement of wise men, especially the Cardinals in consistory;
>
> 3: Has implored the light of the Holy Spirit;
>
> 4: Has ordered public prayer for the aid of the Holy Spirit."¹¹

But this is not true, says St. Alphonsus:

> "Because, although these conditions are

fitting, they are not necessary; for papal infallibility was promised to the Pope and not to his consultors." [12]

"All who hold papal infallibility, must hold that it was given to the Pope and not to the Councils, nor to the Pope after his judgement had been examined, but to the Pope alone. Otherwise, heretics can always object that sufficient examination was lacking to some defined question..." [13]

Therefore, the Pope is infallible:

"When he speaks even aside from a Council:

1: As universal teacher;

2: Who defines ex cathedra

3: Matters of faith or morals, matters, i.e., which are concerned with the law alone, or with some fact connected with law;

4: And when he does this by his supreme power granted to St. Peter and through him to all his successors by Jesus Christ." [14]

But if the Pope is subject to no one in his judgement, how can one be sure that he is not acting rashly and imprudently in defining something of faith and morals? In the mind of Saint Alphonsus, it is precisely here that the negative assistance of the Holy Spirit is operative. It belongs to the very nature of infallibility, according to the Saint, that the Holy Spirit not only aid the Pope so that he define nothing which is against faith or morals, but also that he not use his charism of infallibility rashly or imprudently. Following Suarez' opinion, Saint Alphonsus says:

> "It pertains to the providence of the Holy Spirit...that He will see to it that the Pope never act or decide rashly or imprudently in matters of such importance." [15]

The Pope, however, is not infallible when:

> "1: There is question of a mere doubt of fact which is dependent upon human testimony alone; or
>
> 2: When he speaks as a private doctor." [16]

From this statement of the Saint, one can see that, in his mind, the charism of infallibility involves no new divine revelation made to the Pope. There is not a new truth revealed to the Pope by Almighty God, which he then proposes to the faithful. God simply guides him so that he does not err when he declares that a certain truth is in the deposit of revelation, or that some truth is intimately connected with the deposit of revelation. Thus, when there is question of a doubt of fact, dependent upon human testimony alone, the only way that the Pope could give an infallible pronouncement on the question, would be for God to give the answer by a new public revelation. This He would not do, since public revelation ceased at the death of the last Apostle.[17] If God were to give the Pope the answer by a private revelation, this would not be sufficient, for the charism of infallibility is concerned only with the deposit of public revelation and those things which are intimately connected with it.

Since the Pope is the supreme and infallible ruler in the Church, he, of necessity, has full authority over the Councils, whether they be particular or ecumenical. Such authority over Councils flows just as surely and just as immediately as any other of the papal powers from the Pope's basic supreme authority. Due, however, to the times in which Saint Alphonsus lived, when many men were still strongly defending Conciliarism, the Saint spent much time in each one of his works on papal authority proving that the Pope was above the Council. There was no intrinsic reason either in the nature of papal authority, or of an ecumenical Council why he should have spent more time defending this prerogative of the Pope than e.g. the Pope's universal jurisdiction, but as an apologist, it was his office to answer the major objections of the day. He states quite simply the relationship of authority between the Pope and the General Council:

1: "The Pope alone can legitimately convoke a Council.

2: If a Council is convoked without his authority, but afterwards is ratified by him, the Council becomes legitimate.

3: The Pope can, for grave reasons, depute another to convoke a Council.[18]

4: When the Council is presided over by the Pope who is the head united to the body (that is, to the assembly of Bishops); or when the Council is confirmed by the Pope; then the Council cannot be considered as being superior to the Pope, for otherwise, the Council would not need the authority of the Pope. Besides, if this were true, then the Pope would be conferring authority upon a superior which is absurd.

5: When the Council is considered apart from the Pope, then the Council has no authority at all... because the Council is an assembly of Bishops, but an assembly established under the Pope as head.[19]

6: The Council can be considered as being convoked by the Pope, but then divided from him, so that it is a body separated from its head. In this case, the question is asked, is the Pope above the Council, or the Council above the Pope?"[20]

"The opinion to which we subscribe is this: The Pope is always above the General Council, that is, above all the churches, even collectively taken." [21]

Having stated this basic relationship of authority between the Pope and the general Council, Saint Alphonsus then predicates infallibility of a general Council (which is, of course, convoked and headed by the Supreme Pontiff):

"The Church teaches doctrine to us through the general Councils, and the constant tradition of the faithful has held that the definitions of a general Council are infallible... and truly, it would be a great injustice, indeed, to deny infallibility to the general Councils, since they take the place of the universal Church. If they are able to err in things of faith, then the whole Church would be able to err. If this is true, then we would have to say that God did not care enough about the unity of faith, and yet, He should have cared, since He wished all to be of one faith."[22]

And he gives the reason for the existence of general Councils:

1: They help to make the Bishops more energetic in the suppression of heresies.

2: They serve to reprimand the contumacious.

3: They help to make the Bishops more skilled...in instructing their people.

4: They help to make the papal definitions publicly known everywhere.

5: They help to make the dogmas of faith more diligently held.

6: Sometimes the Pope calls a Council so that through the discussion which is held on some doubt of faith in the Council, he may be more clearly illumined by the Holy Spirit...[23]

7: The Popes after their definitions in no way wait for the confirmation of them by the Councils, so that they might be firm and irrefragable. But they do leave to the Councils the formation of the decrees.[24]

8: (Yet) the Popes in the past have had their condemnations of certain heresies confirmed by the general Councils...in order

> that they might make their own judgement more solemn by having it declared in a general Council; and
>
> 9: That the unbelievers might be completely silenced, i.e. those who would refuse to accept the condemnation of the pope alone, alleging that the Pope had not sufficient knowledge of the case at hand, or did not give sufficient thought to the question..."[25]

Saint Alphonsus also treats several questions which are allied with the concept of papal authority:

I: He treats the general question of succession to the See of Rome by showing that in the case of an illegitimately elected Pope, or of a doubtfully elected Pope, the basic concept of succession to the power of St. Peter has not been destroyed. For perpetual succession to the Chair of Peter, does not demand that the Chair of Peter be always occupied. This is not necessary to the concept of continuous or unbroken succession. For each time the Pope dies, the Chair of Peter is empty. Necessary to the concept of perpetual succession is this: that the Pope elected be chosen _as_ the successor of Saint Peter with the very same authority and powers that Peter had as Vicar of Christ.[26] Thus, Saint Alphonsus says:

> "It makes no difference that in past ages some Pope was illegitimately elected or fraudulently usurped the Pontificate. It is sufficient that he be afterwards accepted by the whole Church, for by such acceptance, he is made the true and legitimate Pontiff.

But if he were never generally accepted, then during the time that he would be holding the Pontificate, the Pontifical See would be empty, as it is at the death of a Pontiff. - In the same way, it makes no difference if in the case of a schism, there would be doubt for a long time as to who was true Pope. One was true, even though he was not sufficiently recognized. But if among the Antipopes, there was no true Pope, in a similar way, the Pontificate would be empty."[27]

II: Treating the question whether or not the Primacy is linked to the Roman See by divine law or human law, Saint Alphonsus leaves the speculative question alone and remarks:

"It is certain after the death of Saint Peter who fixed his Pontificate to the Roman See, that it would not be lawful, nor would it ever become lawful for the universal Church to annex the succession of St. Peter's See to some other Bishop than the Bishop of Rome, by separating the Episcopal power of the city of Rome from the Pontifical power, for it would be interrupting the succession of the Roman Bishop in whom the faithful, following the example of the holy Fathers, have always recognized the successor to the power of St. Peter.

"It does not matter," he adds "that the Popes lived in Avignon for such a long time. For personal residence in Rome is not necessary to exercise true jurisdiction over it. While the Popes were at Avignon, moreover, there was no one else regarded as the Roman Pontiff, except he who dwelt at Avignon."[28]

III: Saint Alphonsus treats the difficult question of a doubtfully elected Pope. He writes:

> "That the pope is above the Council is not to be understood of a doubtful Pope in times of schism, when doubt as to his election has probability, because then everyone must submit to the Council...For then, a general Council has supreme power immediately from God..."[29]

And again:

> "A Council can elect the Pope in case of a doubtful Pope."[30]

And finally:

> "During the time of the fourth and fifth sessions of Constance, the Council was not ecumenical...but as Cardinal Bellarmine says...although the Council without the authority of the Pontiff was not able to define new dogmas of faith, yet it was able, in the time of schism, to provide the Church with a new Pastor when the incumbent is doubtful..."[31]

Today, the opinion that a general Council, during the time of a doubtful Pope, has supreme power immediately from God would not be held - if by supreme power is meant the power that is ordinarily vested in the Supreme Pontiff. However, it does not seem that St. Alphonsus meant "supreme power" in this sense. For following Bellarmine, he holds that a Council at such a time has no power at all to define doctrine. Perhaps all that he meant by "supreme power" was the power to elect a Pope when there was a probable doubt as to the validity of the Pope's election...

Finally, the last question the Saint deals with is the position of a general Council in relation to an heretical Pope. He says:

> "If the Pope ever, as a private person, were to fall into heresy, then at that moment, he would cease to be Pope, because he would then be outside the Church, and as such, would no longer be able to be the head of the Church. In this case, the Church would not depose him, because no one has authority above the Pope. It would simply declare that he had fallen from his pontificate. We have said: 'if the Pope as a private person were to fall into heresy', for the Pope, as Pope, ie. as teaching the whole Church ex cathedra, is not able to teach anything against faith..." [32]

But the Saint teaches that this heresy

> ...must be a question of manifest and external heresy, not of an occult or mental heresy. [33]

And again:

> Then (when he is a manifest and external heretic) the Pope is not deprived of his power by the Council as by a superior, but ...he is immediately despoiled of it by Christ... [34]

In the chapters which follow, many other points will be brought out which will further define the essence of papal authority according to the mind of St. Alphonsus... The epitome of his concept of papal authority given in this chapter is important to show the finis of St. Alphonsus' writings on the Pope. His aim was not to prove per se that the Pope is infallible, or that he has jurisdiction over certain cases, or that he has authority over all bishops, etc. His aim was to prove that this man who is Christ's Vicar upon earth, is vested by Christ with supreme and absolute authority over everyone in Christ's Mystical Body; and that only if this supreme and absolute authority is recognized and accepted by all, can Christ's Church live and progress. With this basic concept in mind, St. Alphonsus' full teaching on papal authority and the proofs he used from Sacred Scripture, the Magisterium, the Fathers and Theologians, and from reason to confirm this teaching can now be examined, and it is hoped, better understood.

NOTES TO CHAPTER III

1. "Constitutio dogmatica I de Ecclesia Christi," cap 3: "De vi et ratione primatus Romani Pontificis" (CL VII, 482 ff; Denziger, 1826 - 1831).
2. R. Corrigan, S.J. The Church and the Nineteenth Century (Milwaukee, 1938) 202.
3. Matthew 28.20; John 16.13
4. Vindiciae contra Justinum Febronium ...(hereafter referred to as Vindiciae) 1 (ODW I, 385).
5. Vindiciae 1, 3 (ODW I, 390 - 391).
6. Vindiciae 7, 4 (ODW I, 431).
7. Vindiciae 1, 3 (ODW I, 390 - 391).
8. Theologia Moralis 6, 959 (OMG IV, 139).
9. Theologia Moralis 3, 931 (OMG II, 334).
10. Vindiciae "Finis Operis" 8 (ODW I, 389).
11. Dissertatio de Romani Pontificis Auctoritate...(hereafter referred to as Dissertatio de Rom. Pont.) 110 (OMG I, 95).
12. Ibidem
13. Verita della Fede 3, 10, 3 (OON 8, 211; ODW I, 345).
14. Verita della Fede 3, 10, 2 (OON 8, 211; ODW I, 345). cf also Dissertatio de Rom. Pont. 110 (OMG I, 93).
15. Dissertatio de Rom. Pont. 110 (OMG I, 95) cf Suarez, De Fide disp. 5, sect 8, n. 11.
16. Verita della Fede 3, 10, 2 (OON 8, 211; ODW I, 345).
17. Council of Trent, Sessio IV (Mansi 33, 22A; Denziger 783). cf. M. Nicalau, J. Salaverri, S. J. Sacrae Theologiae Summa (Madrid, 1950) 1. 750:

> "The thesis (that public revelation ceased at the death of the last Apostle) can be said to be implicitly defined by Trent..."

18. <u>Verita della Fede</u> 3, 10, 2 (OON 8, 178; ODW I, 304). cf. <u>Dissertatio de Rom. Pont.</u> 121 (OMG I, 107).
19. <u>Dissertatio de Rom. Pont.</u> 121 (OMG I, 107). cf. <u>Verita della Fede</u> 3, 10, 2 (OON 8, 178; ODW I, 304).
20. <u>Verita della Fede</u> 3, 10, 2 (OON 8, 178; ODW I, 304).
21. <u>Dissertatio de Rom. Pont.</u> 121 (OMG I, 108).
22. <u>Storia della Eresie</u> 11, 75 (OON 8, 360; ODW II, 442)
23. <u>Vindiciae</u> 7, 17 (ODW I, 439).
24. <u>Vindiciae</u> 11, 5 (ODW I, 448).
25. <u>Vindiciae</u> 11, 4 (ODW I, 448).
26. It is to be understood, of course, that the one chosen either be or be able to be consecrated Bishop by a successor of one of the Apostles.
27. <u>Verita della Fede</u> 3, 8, 9 (OON 8, 176-177; ODW I, 302-303).
28. <u>Verita della Fede</u> 3, 8, 8 (OON 8, 176; ODW I, 302).
29. <u>Dissertatio de Rom. Pont.</u> 121 (OMG I, 107).
30. <u>Verita della Fede</u> 3, 9, 29 (OON 8, 191; ODW I, 321).
31. <u>Verita della Fede</u> 3, 9, 35 (OON 8, 194; ODW I, 326).
32. <u>Vindiciae</u> 8, 8 (ODW I, 445). cf. <u>Verita della Fede</u> 3, 9, 30 (OON 8, 192); ODW I, 321).
33. <u>Dissertatio de Rom. Pont.</u> 121 (OMG I, 107).
34. Ibid, cf. also <u>Verita della Fede</u> 3, 9, 37 (OON 8, 195; ODW I, 326).

CHAPTER V

SAINT ALPHONSUS' USE OF THE MAGISTERIUM OF THE CHURCH TO ESTABLISH PAPAL AUTHORITY

PART I: AN EVALUATION OF SAINT ALPHONSUS' USE OF THE MAGISTERIUM

The next source after Sacred Scripture which Saint Alphonsus uses to establish papal authority is the teaching of both the Popes and the councils. Though Saint Alphonsus does not use the term, this is obviously an appeal to the Magisterium of the Church, the Magisterium as it is expressed by its two principal organs, the Popes and the General Councils.[1] At times, the Saint will also appeal to the teaching of some particular or provincial Council to confirm a point, especially if that council has had the special approbation of the Pope, or is itself held under the Pope, as were the particular councils of Rome.[2] Though Saint Alphonsus does not attribute infallibility to these particular councils, as he does to the General Councils,[3] still in the mind of the Saint, these particular councils can reflect the traditional teaching of the Church, since they are made up of some of the bishops, who in turn make up part of the general Magisterium of the Church. And if their teaching is in accord with the teachings of the Pope and the General Councils, then it certainly can be appealed to, at least as a confirmatory argument.

In his <u>Vindiciae</u>, Saint Alphonsus goes into the question of just what the cumulative authority of the bishops scattered throughout the world would be, i.e., the authority of the ordinary Magisterium of the Church (though, again this term as such is not found in the works of Saint Alphonsus). He remarks that Febronius errs when he says that the bishops are a body only when they are joined together in council, and that, therefore, they are infallible only when they are gathered together as a body in a General Council. The Saint quotes Duval and a statement of the Faculty of Paris in 1664 to prove that it is of faith that the Church is infallible not only when it is joined in an ecumenical Council, but even when it is scattered throughout the world. From this, Saint Alphonsus concludes that when the majority of the bishops, either in council or out of council, accept an opinion which is in accord with the judgment of the Pope, then that teaching represents a dogma of the faith.[4] Thus, in the mind of Alphonsus, if a particular Council of Bishops accept a teaching which is in accord with the judgment of the Pope, this is, at least, an indication of what the teaching of the whole Magisterium is. It is in this way that the Saint uses the authority of the particular councils.

In his use of the Magisterium of the Church to establish papal authority, Saint Alphonsus does not go over the same ground which he covered in his proofs from Sacred Scripture, so that the quotations from the Magisterium merely prove again the very same points he already proved from the Scripture texts. To do this would not give any further precision to his basic teaching. Consequently, he takes for granted that the points he handled under the Sacred Scripture proofs are sufficiently established, and he uses this new source of tradition, the Magisterium, to emphasize a different phase of his teaching which will result in a deeper and more conclusive exposition of his whole thesis. In his proofs from Scripture, the Saint concentrated on showing how the Sacred texts proved again and again that Christ conferred authority on Peter alone. He showed also that a proper understanding of the same texts demanded that Peter have a successor who would hold the same power over the Church that Peter himself held. That successor is the Pope of Rome. He points out briefly that the Magisterium also attests to these two facts, but then proceeds to show how the Magisterium is basically concerned with the fact of the Pope's supremacy in the Church, and the powers of ruling, judging, and teaching which necessarily flow from his supremacy. In the Sacred Scripture proofs, the emphasis was primarily on Peter, and the fact that he had to have a successor. In the proofs from the Magisterium, the emphasis changes, and centers around the successor of Peter to show that he is truly supreme in the Church and holds the supreme powers of ruling and judging and teaching all in the Church. Such a change of emphasis brings the truth of the full doctrine of papal authority into even greater relief.

In handling this source of tradition, Saint Alphonsus simply points out the fact of the Magisterium's attestation to the truth of papal supremacy. He is not here concerned with theological speculation about the very nature of the supreme power nor about the intrinsic nature of the powers which flow from papal supremacy. The Magisterium itself is not concerned explicitly with these matters. It merely states the general truth that the Pope is supreme in the Church and has certain powers inherent in his very supremacy. This truth is stated as a teaching of the whole Church, i.e., of the Pope, and of the bishops in union with the Pope gathered in General Councils, and even in provincial Councils. It was Saint Alphonsus' task to gather a sufficient amount of testimonies from the Magisterium in every age of the Church to show conclusively that this is a truth the Church has always taught, and that there was never a time in the history of the Church that she taught a different doctrine. In his treatment of the Fathers and Theologians as a witness of tradition which prove papal authority, the Saint points out how these Fathers and Theologians used theological reasoning and speculation to establish papal power more firmly. Such reasoning and speculation is not necessary in the Magisterium. The very fact of its attestation to papal supremacy is, in the mind of Saint Alphonsus, sufficient proof of his thesis.

These observations become quite evident when one reads the works of Alphonsus on papal authority. The appeal to the Magisterium is one of the strongest and most lengthy proofs that he employs. From his extensive use of such a source, one can easily conclude that the Saint accorded great importance to this organ of tradition. In the mind of this writer, Saint Alphonsus' stress on the teaching of the Magisterium to prove his basic premise is good indication that Alphonsus saw the Magisterium as the ultimate source of all true tradition. It is indeed theological anachronism to attribute to a writer both terms and precisions of theological thought which evolved only many years after the death of the writer. But in studying a man's work, one can quite often see glimmerings of such terms and concepts. Thus it is with Alphonsus' work on papal authority. The respect in which he held the teachings of the Popes and the councils, and the prominence which he gave to those teachings in his writings lead one to see indications, at least, of a distinction between active and passive tradition, and also of a concept which flows immediately from this distinction, the fact of the Magisterium of the Church being the living voice of tradition. It seems that in the Saint's mind, tradition was not just the aggregate of revealed truths which in the course of time had found their way into non-inspired writings. Such a concept of tradition would suffice as a remote rule of Faith, but not as a norm of Faith. Thus the writings of Saint Alphonsus suggest that though the truth itself can be distinguished from the very handing down of that truth, still it cannot be entirely separated from the teaching and transmitting of these truths. For just as the Apostles received truths from Christ and the Holy Spirit and handed down or taught these truths, so the Magisterium of the Church in every age hands down and teaches these same truths which it has received from the Apostles. Therefore, the Church has received the revelation from God through His Apostles, and by its Magisterium teaches this very same revelation today. This is what is known in modern theological language as active tradition. For the Church is the deposit and the guardian of revelation so that she may be the propounder and teacher of this same revelation. She is never a quiescent receiver or deposit -- she is the teaching receiver. She possesses and teaches today and every day the complete revelation which Christ and the Holy Spirit gave to His Apostles. Thus, the Magisterium of the Church is the infallible, living, indefectible propounder of the whole of tradition. Anything that it has proposed and proposes today as a revealed doctrine, is a revealed doctrine, and this is the only revealed doctrine. Therefore, the Magisterium of the Church in any age is the living voice of tradition. It says what has been handed down, because it possesses what has been handed down. Thus the most powerful theological proof that one can present is a presentation of what the Magisterium of the Church has taught down through the centuries. For when one presents the teaching of the Magisterium, by that very fact one presents the correct interpretation of the Sacred Scripture texts and the true doctrine of the great Fathers and Doctors of the Church. A Scripture text can be misinterpreted. A Father or Theologian can err. But the Living Voice of Tradition, the Magisterium, cannot wrongly interpret Sacred Scripture, and is unable to accept any error of a Father or Theologian. For as the Teacher of Christ's Church, it and it alone is infallible, and as such, is indefectible.

In this writer's opinion, indications of such an attitude toward the Magisterium of the Church are certainly to be found in Alphonsus' writings on papal authority. In his Verita della Fede, for example, where the Saint treats of the infallibility of tradition, he gives first a definition of tradition. He writes:

> "Traditions are truths first communicated to the Apostles by Jesus Christ or the Holy Spirit, and then handed down by the Apostles to their disciples, and thus communicated and passed on from hand to hand under the direction of the Holy Spirit without any interruption to our own day.[5]"

Then the saint goes on to say why tradition is necessary:

> The necessity of traditions can be especially recognized from the fact that without them, the Church would never have known with certitude that the Scriptures exist, what are the genuine books, what is the correct version, and what is the true sense of the text...[6]

He gives next the reason for the incorruptibility of tradition:

> "...One might ask 'are not the traditions subject to corruption?' I answer: even the Scriptures are subject to corruption. However, Divine Providence which assists the Church, has not permitted, nor will it ever permit God's word to be corrupted in the hand of the Church which holds the deposit of the word of God.[7]"

And finally, Alphonsus states the position of the Church (i.e., the Magisterium of the Church) in relation to tradition:

> "For tradition to be a certain rule of faith, it should be infallibly clear that is is divine, but this can only be clear from the authority of the Church, which under the guiding hand of the Holy Spirit, and on the promise of Christ, can distinguish the false from the true traditions. In this she cannot err..[8]"

It is especially these insights of Saint Alphonsus into the concept of tradition, added to his deeply respectful attitude toward the teachings of the Magisterium found throughout his works on papal authority, that leads one to see definite indications of the concepts already discussed.[9]

It has been noted that Saint Alphonsus' use of the Magisterium as a source to prove papal authority comprises the teachings of both the Popes and the councils. In his use of papal teaching to attest to the truth of papal supremacy, one is able to see here, too, indications of theological precisions which would be expressed in their fullness only after many more years of evolution. There are indications of a distinction between the science of Apologetics and Fundamental Theology. There is a glimmering of the truth which Pope Pius IX so clearly and succinctly expressed in the few words "La tradizione son'io. -- I am tradition."[10] There is, finally in the Saint's very use of the testimony of the Popes, a hint of the concept of the ordinary Magisterium of the Pope.

The indications of a distinction between Apologetics and Fundamental Theology are found in Saint Alphonsus' reason for using the papal teachings to prove the supreme authority of the Popes. He states that the opponents of papal power refuse to accept the testimonies of the Popes because the Popes are testifying here in their own behalf and, therefore, their testimony has no value."[11] Saint Alphonsus has several answers to this objection. In his first answer he indicates the distinction between Apologetics and Fundamental Theology. He writes:

> "...but they (the definitions of the Popes) have full authority for me and for many others, since they are sentences pronounced by the Vicars of Jesus Christ who were established by Christ in their age as the Teachers of the Universal Church.[12]"

This first answer to the objection of the adversaries has no apologetic value whatever. Surely,

Saint Alphonsus who was a trained lawyer and skilled in seeing the force of an argument for particular opponents must have understood this. The answer has, however, very powerful theological value, and it is the contention of this writer that the Saint meant it to be taken in a theological sense only. To Alphonsus and other theologians who were interested in developing the whole concept of papal authority, and who believed that the Pope was the Vicar of Christ and the teacher of the universal Church, any declaration of the Pope on papal authority would be a further precision in their knowledge of papal supremacy, and of the whole science of fundamental theology or ecclesiology. For their science deals in revelation, and the things connected with revelation. When the Pope as Vicar of Christ teaches the whole Church, he is giving these Theologians, especially, a further understanding of revelation. His statements, therefore, are the most powerful part of their whole treatise on papal authority, and in Saint Alphonsus' words "have full authority -- tutta l'autorita." Thus Alphonsus has indicated that a fundamental theologian's proof is not necessarily an apologist's proof. The basic reason for this must be that there are two different sciences involved, each having its own _objectum formale quo_ and _quod_. The fundamental theologian deals in revelation -- this is his _objectum formale quod_. He uses faith guided by reason -- this is his _objectum formale quo_. On the other hand, the apologist deals in the motives of credibility as his _objectum formale quod_, and uses reason alone as his _objectum formale quo_. Had not Saint Alphonsus understood something of this difference, the answer which he gave to the adversaries of papal supremacy would have simply been an _argumentum in circulo vitioso_.[13]

The second answer which Alphonsus gives to this same objection of the opponents of papal power is a purely apologetic answer. He says that simply weighing the relative positions of the Popes and the opponents of the Popes, one would surely be wiser to accept the teachings of the Popes on this matter, since they are recognized by so many as the great teachers, rather than the teachings of a few individuals like Maimburg and Dupin and Launoy.[14] If it is a question of accepting one man's opinion rather than another's, then the Popes, even though they are testifying in their own defense, certainly have the edge on authority. He states:

> "...does the authority of Maimburg, Dupin, and Launoy have greater weight than the authority of so many Roman Pontiffs whom the General Councils have called and have considered the successors of Peter, the Vicars of Christ, the organs of the Holy Spirit, the heads of the Christian world, and teachers with full and supreme power over the universal Church?[15]"

Such a preponderance of authority compared to the little authority of the opponents of papal supremacy would be a true motive of credibility for accepting the testimony of the Popes.

Saint Alphonsus' third answer to the objection of the adversaries that the Popes' testimonies with regard to their supremacy have no value because they are made in the Popes' own behalf contains a hint at least of the truth enunciated by Pope Pius IX when he said, "I am tradition". By these words the Pope meant that as the teacher of all the faithful who, because he is teacher, must hold within himself the whole deposit of revelation so that he might impart that revelation to others, he is the one who can say what traditions are; he is the one who is the witness of true tradition. As supreme head of the Magisterium he is, above all others, the Living Voice of Tradition. He can say what the true revelation is, because he holds the deposit of all revelation, both from the inspired sources and from the witnesses of the non-inspired writings. Saint Alphonsus observes:

> "Although the definition of a judge whose very judging-power has been called into doubt does not seem to prove that he is judge, still it cannot be denied that at least the many definitions of the Popes add great weight to our opinion, since it can surely be said that these Popes would not have so easily uttered these definitions unless their opinions had been universally received in the Church.[16]"

This answer of Alphonsus has more than just apologetic value. It indicates that the Pope, who is accepted by the whole Church as having the right authoritatively to teach his own supremacy, is looked upon by the Saint as the living voice of the belief or the tradition of the Church; is looked upon, indeed, as the one in whom the whole of tradition is summed up. For if the Church accepts the fact that the Pope teaches his own supremacy as a dogma always believed in the Church, then it must be that the Pope is able to do this because he holds the whole deposit of revelation in his own hands; it must be that he himself is tradition. Otherwise, the whole Church would have to be the teacher, and the Pope merely the one who assents to the belief and traditions of the Church. For he who basically holds the doctrine must be the primary teacher of that doctrine.

It has been stated that Saint Alphonsus' very use of the testimonies of the Popes to prove papal supremacy gives indication of a recognition of what today is called the 'ordinary magisterium of the Pope.' The term of course is much later than Alphonsus. (Indeed, the first document coming from the Holy See that this writer could find which used the term as such was Pope Pius XII's Humani Generis![17] The first theologian found using the term was Jean Michael Vacant in his Etudes Theologiques sur les Constitutions du Concile du Vatican.[18] The concept is earlier. It is found as early as Bellarmine who states that the Pope must be heard obediently by all the faithful when he establishes some doubtful matter, whether he is able to err or not.[19] The question of the authority of the statements of the Pope which are not ex cathedra was not specifically treated by Alphonsus. But his attitude in using the testimony of the Popes suggests what he thought of that authority. In quoting the Popes to prove basic supreme power, the Saint does not examine each of the testimonies to see whether they fulfill the requirements which he himself laid down for an ex cathedra statement. The very fact that the Popes were fulfilling their duties as teachers of the universal Church sufficed in Alphonsus' mind to give their statements great authority. From this attitude of the Saint it can be concluded that he recognized a teaching power in the Popes outside the use of their personal charism of infallibility, whereby they were able, because of this very office, to teach all the faithful at all times. This power was something inherent in the very supremacy of the Popes. It was ordinary to their office. And as the divinely appointed teachers of the whole Church, the Popes were to be heard with great respect and their teachings, even though not personally infallible, were to be accepted with great obedience. Thus, Saint Alphonsus, even by his attitude, has hinted at a doctrine that has not been evolved in its fullness even in our own day, although Pope Pius XII has given it great impetus by his great work in Humani Generis.[20]

Having shown the validity of the papal testimonies to prove papal supremacy, Saint Alphonsus goes on to show the strength of the arguments from the General Councils to establish this same point. Arguing first against the Conciliarists in general, and Febronius in paritcular, who held that the supreme power together with the prerogative of infallibility in defining questions of faith was promised only to the General Councils and not to Peter and his successors, the Saint says:

> "If I prove that the General Councils themselves attributed supreme power to the Pope, who can deny that the Pope is infallible and superior to the Councils? But Febronius will say, 'Where in the Councils will you find this proposition that the Pope is infallible and superior to the Councils?' This proposition, I grant, is not found in any Council expressed in these specific terms; but many Councils say that the Pope is the Head, holding power above the whole Church; they say that the Pope is the Vicar of Christ, immediately made so by Christ Himself, and therefore, they say, all things are to be held which are defined by him; they say that the Pope has supreme power over the whole Church, and therefore, all questions of faith are to be decided by him; they say that the definitions of the Popes are not able to be changed, since the Pope

is the organ of the Holy Spirit; they say that there can be no recourse from the sentence of a Pope to another superior; they say that outside the case of heresy the Pope is subject in no way whatever to the judgement of another power; they say finally that it is illicit to appeal from the Pope to a Council, but that it is good to appeal from the Council to the Pope.

Having established these things who can say that the Pope is fallible and is subject to a Council?[21]"

It will be part of the task of this Chapter to point out what Councils Saint Alphonsus used to prove the points he so succinctly summed up here.

Alphonsus' next point in proving the strength of the argument from the General Councils is to prove against the Protestants that the General Councils are infallible. He says that the Church teaches doctrine through the General Councils, and for this reason it has been the perpetual tradition of all the faithful that the definitions of such Councils are infallible. He goes on to remark that Luther and Calvin and their followers held that the General Councils were not infallible. But so to deny infallibility to the General Councils, says Alphonsus, is to do a great injury to these Councils. For they take the place of the whole Church, and if they can err in things of faith, then the whole Church can err. And if this is true, he says, then one would have to say with the atheists that God had not sufficiently taken care of the unity of faith, and He should have taken care of this unity, since He wished all to be of one faith. From this the Saint concludes that it must be held de fide that the General Councils are not able to err in those things which pertain to faith and morals.[22]

The Saint proves his thesis that the General Councils are infallible by an appeal to Sacred Scripture and the Fathers of the Church. His first text from Scripture is <u>The Spirit of Truth shall teach you all truth</u>,[23] combined with, <u>And I shall ask the Father, and He will give you another Advocate to dwell with you forever, the Spirit of truth</u>, etc?[24] From these two texts the Saint argues that Christ promised His Apostles and His whole Church that the Holy Spirit would remain in the Church to teach the truths of faith not only to the Apostles (since they would not remain in this mortal life forever) but also to the Bishops who would succeed them.[25] Therefore, if the Holy Spirit was going to remain with the bishops to teach them all truth, then surely, when they collectively teach a truth in union with their chief Bishop, the Bishop of Rome, they must be infallible. Otherwise, it would have to be said that the Holy Spirit teaches error. This conclusion is not in Saint Alphonsus, it is simply taken for granted by him as a necessary consequence to his argumentation.

Alphonsus then appeals to a text of St. Matthew which he has already used to establish that the Pope is the successor of St. Peter to prove now that the General Councils are infallible. He establishes two points from the text, <u>And behold, I am with you all days, even to the consummation of the world?</u>[26] The first point is this: If Christ is going to stay with His Church forever, then it can never fall into error; and his second point: Fathers of the Church such as Athanasius, Epiphanius, Cyprian, Augustine, and Gregory have always held that the General Councils take the place of the whole Church. If the Church cannot err because Christ is always with it, then neither can the General Councils err which take the place of the Church?[27]

Saint Alphonsus' appeal to the Fathers of the Church to confirm his thesis is rather brief. He says simply:

> "The Holy Fathers such as St. Gregory of Nazienzus, St. Basil, St. Cyril, St. Ambrose, St. Athanasius, St. Augustine, and St. Leo, regarded all those as heretics who fought against dogmas defined by the General Councils.[28]"

With the authority of Sacred Scripture and the Fathers of the Church to back him up, Saint Alphonsus then proceeds to show how an objection which the Protestants raise against the infallibility of the General Councils has no force. They say that the only duty of the General Council is to seek truth. The solution of all doubts comes entirely from Sacred Scripture. Therefore, a definition does not depend upon a majority vote of the Fathers of the Councils, but upon what is more consistent with the sense of Sacred Scripture. To have it any other way is to put the authority of the General Councils above the authority of Sacred Scripture, and this, they say, is blasphemy.[29] In answer to this, Saint Alphonsus observes:

> "The Word of God, both written (Sacred Scripture) and non-written (Tradition) is certainly to be placed before any Council. But the Councils do not make the Word of God. They declare what are the true Sacred Scriptures, and what are the true Traditions, and what their true sense is.[30]"

The Saint's final step in establishing the infallibility of the General Councils is to show how reason itself demands that the General Councils be infallible. He writes:

> "If the General Councils were able to err, there would be no firm judgement in the Church whereby discords about dogmas could be settled. Moreover, we would never be able to say of any heresy that it is condemned or indeed, that it is a heresy... Finally, all the Councils would have committed an intolerable error by proposing as articles of faith those things which the Councils themselves are not sure are true or false..."[31]

It will have been noticed in all Saint Alphonsus' proofs for the infallibility of the General Councils that he studiously avoided any reference to the personal infallibility of the Popes. The reason for this becomes quite obvious when one realizes that the Saint was writing a work against the Protestants who denied all authority to the Pope. If he tried to prove immediately that this Pope, whom they excoriated, was infallible, he would not even be heard. He had much better chance of a hearing if he concentrated on the General Councils, because they were recognized by some Protestants, at least, as having some authority. This is good Apologetics -- to seek common ground with one's adversaries and to talk from there. It need scarcely be said, because of all that has already been written in this work, that Saint Alphonsus' full thought on the infallibility of the Councils was that they were infallible insofar and to the extent that they were in union with the Pope, who is their infallible head. If he could once persuade the Protestants to accept the fact of the infallibility of the General Councils, it would then be an easy task to show them, as he showed Febronius, how the very General Councils themselves ascribed supreme and infallible power to the Pope.

Having seen how Saint Alphonsus established the validity of the testimony of the Popes and the strength of the testimony from the General Councils to prove papal sovereignty, the relationship which the Saint saw between these two organs of the Magisterium can now be pointed out. If Alphonsus had said nothing at all about the relationship between the teaching of the Popes and the General Councils, the very way in which he used these two sources and the things which he quoted from the councils especially would themselves show this relationship. He constantly shows the Popes declaring a doctrine, and the councils reiterating and accepting that same doctrine. As it is, however, it will not be necessary to draw any conclusions from his use of these sources, for he himself in both his <u>Verita della Fede</u> and in his <u>Vindiciae contra Febronium</u> has given a rather detailed treatment of the relationship which exists between the teachings of the Popes and the teachings of the General Councils. In these two works, Saint Alphonsus treats this question in answer to an objection of the opponents of papal authority who say that if it is true that the Pope is personally infallible, then the General Councils are of no use whatever. Against this position the Saint writes in his <u>Verita della Fede</u>:

> "...By no means are the Councils useless. They are good for many things. They help make decrees which have been sanctioned by the Councils to be more freely accepted by the people...They help the Bishops to be more fully instructed in a doctrine and the full reasons for decrees so that these same Bishops may more easily teach the defined

> truths to their own flocks. They help to silence those who murmur against the definitions of the Popes. They likewise help to examine further some points which have not yet been defined nor sufficiently discussed...[32]"

And in his <u>Vindiciae</u>, answering the same objection brought forth now by Febronius, the Saint adds several more advantages of General Councils. He says that they make the bishops more energetic in their work of repressing heresies; they help to make papal definitions publicly known everywhere; and finally, that the discussions in the councils help the Pope himself to come to a clearer knowledge of some doubt of faith. The Saint sees the General Councils as an instrument of the Holy Spirit Who uses them and the discussions held in them to enlighten the Pope in some problem of faith.[33]

One last point of relationship between the Popes and the General Councils is brought out by Saint Alphonsus in answer to still another objection of Febronius, who held that the very fact that the General Councils discussed things already defined by the Popes proves that the papal definitions have no solidity or binding force unless they are accepted by the General Councils. If this is not true, says Febronius, why should the councils even discuss things defined by the Popes?[34] In answer to Febronius, Alphonsus has written:

> "The things that have been defined by the Pope are discussed because the Pope both wishes and commands that they be discussed, not so that the truth about a particular definition may be found, but so that the truth which is already found may be

made more clear and more manifest to all. Even schools of dogma examine those things which have already been defined by the Church, not indeed to look into the truth of the dogma, but to illustrate it further, and to make it more clear. The Councils simply did the very same thing..."[351]

Thus, in the mind of Saint Alphonsus, the relationship between the two organs of the Magisterium, the Popes and the General Councils, is a necessary and close relationship. The councils are, in a sense, the mind of the Pope. They serve to clarify doubtful points of doctrine so that he may more intelligently define them. The councils are the arm of the Pope. They confirm, strengthen, implement, and complement his teachings. And finally, the councils are the solemn voice of the Pope, repeating his doctrine clearly to the whole world through the bishops who have gathered in council. The relationship between the infallibility of the Pope and the infallibility of the General Councils with the questions surrounding this relationship, will be left to another Chapter where the Saint will treat the thought of the great Fathers and Theologians of the Church and some of the speculative questions which they brought up.

It has been pointed out thus far that Saint Alphonsus uses the Magisterium, i.e., the Popes and the General Councils, and at times, some particular councils, to attest to the fact of basic papal supremacy; that in the use of this Magisterium, Saint Alphonsus hints at the theological distinctions between passive and active tradition and at the concept of the Magisterium as being the Living Voice of Tradition; that in his use of the papal testimonies, there are indications that he saw a real distinction between Fundamental Theology and the science of Apologetics, that he saw the Popes as the summation of all tradition, and that he understood something of the idea behind the modern term "ordinary magisterium of the Pope"; that he recognized and proved the validity of papal testimony and the strength of the teaching of the General Councils to establish papal authority; and finally, that there was in the mind of Alphonsus a very real relationship between the two organs of the Magisterium, the Popes and the General Councils. Now before seeing what quotations of the Magisterium Saint Alphonsus used to attest to the fact of basic papal supremacy and some of its inherent powers, perhaps it would be well to discuss here just what contribution Saint Alphonsus made to the science of positive theology in his treatment of the Magisterium as a source to prove his teaching on papal authority. This question must ultimately arise in studying the thought of any man. For all the great Doctors and Theologians of the Church handled the same sources of tradition. It was their peculiar genius in the use of these sources which impressed their personality on the traditional texts and enriched the whole field of theology. Especially must this be said of the Doctors who are the officially approved teachers of the Universal Church. By the way in which they handled the sources of Tradition, they added something to the whole content of the Church's teaching, and the Church is richer in the understanding of its own doctrine because of their thoughts and writings. This is true also of each particular doctrine which the genius of these men touched. Any doctrine which they treated has taken on new life, deeper meaning, broader aspects, and has been given greater precision because of the individual writer's personal handling of the very same sources of tradition handled by so many others before him. If such is not true of a writer, then he has merely compiled a handbook on some particular point in theology, and does not seem to deserve the title 'Doctor' or 'teacher' of the Universal Church. What then did Saint Alphonsus contribute to the science of positive theology in his use of the traditional sources to prove papal authority? How did his peculiar genius impress his personality on those texts of tradition so that they took on a new and deeper life? Surely, to say that he who has been named a Doctor of the Universal Church was merely a gatherer or compiler of texts would not seem sufficient. Or to call him simply the "echo of Tradition" in the sense that he merely voiced tradition and contributed nothing of himself or his genius to the riches of the Church's doctrine would not seem great reason for calling him 'Doctor' or for Pope Pius IX singling out his works on papal authority in the very conferring of this title.[36] It seems that more must be said, and it is this writer's opinion that more can be said of Alphonsus' contribution to theology in his use of the sources.

It has already been brought out how Saint Alphonsus in the use of the Fathers to interpret texts of Sacred Scripture quotes many, many of the Fathers, each with a slightly different nuance of thought, so that at the end of the quoting, a much fuller and deeper understanding of the Fathers' interpretation of a Scripture text is had than if only one or two Fathers were quoted to bring out the essential or basic notion. In the Saint's use of the Magisterium, the peculiar genius which he brought to the handling of the texts and which gave the texts deeper and fuller meaning can only be described as great "Catholic-mindedness" -- a profound appreciation and a deep respect for the teachings of the Catholic Church, of the Church which has been made by Christ the Teacher of all mankind. What such "Catholic-mindedness" effected in Saint Alphonsus' use of the testimonies from the Popes and the General Councils is this: His own position and own thoughts as writer are almost completely hidden, and as a result, the teaching of the Magisterium is made to stand out in great relief, and is presented in almost startling clarity as the one great norm of orthodoxy. The Saint's own teaching and the teaching of the opponents of papal authority are examined in the one light of the testimonies of the Infallible Teacher. They stand or fall insofar as they agree or disagree with the teachings of the great Teacher. One is reminded of the attitude of the councils of the past whose norm was: "Peter has spoken through Leo, or through Agatho -- the case is finished." Saint Alphonsus, bringing the teaching of the Magisterium into such relief shows Christ and Peter speaking through the Magisterium, and for him, too, the case is finished.

Around the testimonies of the Magisterium, Saint Alphonsus unobtrusively weaves his own thought and remarks -- so unobtrusively, indeed, that at first glance all one sees is the teaching of the Popes and the councils. His own explanation of that teaching, or a further precision of thought gathered from that teaching, or a necessary conclusion pointed out from the words of a Pope or a General Council, all seem to fade into the teaching of the Magisterium itself. This, of course, was the aim of the Saint -- to so present the testimony of the Magisterium, the Living Voice of Tradition, that his readers would see and hear only its voice, attesting over and over again to the truth of papal supremacy and to the powers inherent in that supremacy. The fact that he, the writer, marshalled these texts in logical form and gave them precise applications goes by almost unnoticed. Thus, Saint Alphonsus in his use of the Magisterium is always in the background, seemingly never showing himself, and yet quietly insisting on the truths which he shows the Living Voice of Tradition to teach -- insisting upon them, and showing them in such a way that to deny these truths is to deny the very foundation upon which the Church is built: Sacred Scripture, authority, and the authoritative voice of the past. And he goes further and points out how the opponents of his teaching who have appealed to these same sources have misused them and with dishonesty have educed half-truths from sources which he shows utterly deny their position. Thus the personality which Saint Alphonsus impressed upon the testimonies of the Magisterium was a great Catholic personality. His peculiar genius lay in so using his catholicity that the pages in his works which prove papal authority from the Magisterium do just what he wanted them to do -- they state: "Here is the doctrine of the Living Mystical Christ. The case is finished." Such a use of the testimonies of the Popes and the General Councils is, in this writer's opinion, a valuable contribution to the riches of Catholic Theology.

NOTES TO CHAPTER V, PART I

1. St. Alphonsus does, however, use the term "Church" in the sense of the authoritative or teaching part of the Church, i.e. the Popes and the General Councils. In this sense, the term "Church" and the "Magisterium of the Church" would mean one and the same thing. See Vindiciae 7, 13 (ODW I, 436), and many, many other places of Alphonsus' works.

2. Thus, for example, the Saint appeals to the III Council of Rome in 501 held under Pope St. Symmachus.

3. St. Alphonsus' proof for the infallibility of the General Councils will be treated later on in this chapter.

4. Vindiciae 7, 15 (ODW I, 438).

5. Verita della Fede 3, 6, 30 (OON 8, 168; ODW I, 292).

6. Verita della Fede 3, 6, 33 (OON 8, 169; ODW I, 294).

7. Verita della Fede 3, 6, 34 (OON 8, 170; ODW I, 294).

8. Verita della Fede 3, 6, 36 (OON 8, 170; ODW I, 295).

9. On this question of the relationship between the Church and Tradition, and the distinction between active and passive Tradition, see: J. B. Cardinal Franzelin, Tractatus de Divinia Traditione et Scriptura (Rome, 1882).
George Agius, Tradition and the Church (Stratford, Boston, 1928).
W. Gurghardt, S.J., "The Catholic Concept of Tradition in the Light of Modern Theological Thought" CTSA Proceedings, (New York, 1951) 42 - 75.
A. Michel, "Tradition" DTC, 15/1 (1946) 1252 - 1350.

10. Such was Pope Pius IX's reply to Cardinal Guidi. At least this is what the Cardinal said the Pope replied to him. See F. Mourret, Le Concile du Vatican (Paris, 1919) 299.
See also R. Aubert, Le Ponfificat de Pie IX (Paris, Bloud and Gay, 1952) 354.

11. Verita della Fede 3, 9, 13 (OON 8, 183; ODW I, 311).

12. Ibid.

13. On this distinction between Apologetics and Fundamental Theology, see:
E. Burke, C.S.P. "The Scientific Teaching of Theology in the Seminary" CTSA Proceedings (New York, 1949) 129 - 173.
M. J. Congar, "Theologie" DTC, 15/1 (1946) 342 - 502.

14. Louis Maimburg (1610 - 1686), was a celebrated and learned French ecclesiastic. He entered the Society of Jesus in 1626, but after writing a defense of the liberties of the Gallican Church, Traite historique de l'etablissement et des prerogatives de l'eglise de Rome, he had to quit the Society on order of the Pope. The King of France gave him a pension, and he returned to the Abbey of St. Victor in Paris and there pursued his historical studies. Though he was an ardent Gallican, he was just as ardent a foe of Jansenism. His Traite historique...was condemned by a brief of Pope Innocent XI.
J. Carreyre, "Maimbourg" DTC, 9/2 (1927) 1656 - 1661.

Jean de Launoy (1603 - 1678) was born at Valdecie. He took his doctorate in theology in 1636 at Navarre, and was ordained priest the same year. In 1643, he was made one of the Royal Censors whose duties were to suppress books in favor of Jansenism and Arnauld. In 1648, he was expelled from the University of Navarre for holding that a priest is not obliged to say his office every day, since it is only a pious custom. After leaving Navarre, he continued to make his home in Paris where he published a great amount of books on history and ecclesiastical discipline. His complete works comprise ten volumes (edited by Abbey Granet, 1731 - 1733).

Theologically, Launoy was interested in the study of the authority and the infallibility of the Pope, the Immaculate Conception, and the Assumption of the Blessed Virgin Mary, and the Sacraments.

Of interest in this work, is his thought on the infallibility and the authority of the Pope. Launoy was a Gallican, and as such, fought vehemently against the infallibility and the absolute authority of the Pope. According to him, the General Council, and not the Pope, was supreme in the Church.

J. Carreyre, "Launoy" DTC, 9/1 (1926) 2 - 6.

Louis-Ellies Dupin (1657 - 1719), was a French theologian who took his doctorate at the Sorbonne in 1684. He started writing as a very young man, and published many works in his day. His theological theories in his Novelle Bibliotheque des auteurs ecclesiastiques gained him a formidable enemy in the great Bossuet, who finally had his Novelle Bibliotheque...condemned by the Archbishop of Paris in 1696.

Although Dupin signed the famous cas-de-conscience of Arnauld, he was not a real Jansenist. He was a follower and disciple of Launoy, and so was a firm Gallican. The summation of his Gallican theories can be found in his commentary on the Four Articles of the French Clergy, his Traite de la puissance ecclesiastique et temporelle (1707).

See also E. Preclin, E. Jarry, Les Luttes Politiques et Doctrinales aux XVIIe et XVIII Siecles (Paris, Bloud & Gay, 1956) (Fliche-Martin, Histoire de L'Eglise, 19) See index for references.

15. Verita della Fede 3, 9, 18 (OON 8, 186; ODW I, 314)

16. Dissertatio de Rom. Pont. 125 (OMG I, 111)

17. AAS, 42 (1950) 561 - 577. The writer of this work has examined all the documents in F. Cavalerra's Thesaurus Doctrinae Ecclesiae (Beauschesne, Paris, 1936) treating of the teaching power of the Pope, and he did not find the term "ordinary magisterium of the Pope" used once in all the documents examined. In the major documents of the Popes after 1936 which this writer examined in the AAS, he could not find the term used until Pope Pius XII's Humani Generis.

18. J. M. Vacant, Etudes Theologiques sur les Constitutions du Concile du Vatican (Paris, 1895) 2, 91.

19. R. Cardinal Bellarmine, De Romano Pontifice, 1581, 4, 2 (Naples, 1856, 477).

20. The literature on this concept of the ordinary magisterium of the Pope is indeed vast, especially since Pope Pius XII's Humani Generis. Father Gustave Weigel, in an article in the Theological Studies, 12 (1952), "Commentaries on Humani Generis" 520 - 549, lists 96 articles commenting on Humani Generis. Because of the central message of this Encyclical, i.e. the ordinary teaching power and value of this teaching power, each of these 96 articles would have had to at least mention this central fact, and comment on it in some way.
See also:
J. Cardinal Franzelin, De Divina Traditione et Scriptura (Rome, 1882).

E. Dublanchy, "Infallibilite du Pape" DTC, 7/2 (1927) 1638 - 1717.
E. Bernard, "Doctrinal Value of the Ordinary Teaching of the Holy Father" CTSA Proceedings (New York, 1951) 78 - 107.
L. Choupin, Valeur des decisions du Saint Siege (Paris, 1912) pages 15 - 17 are of special interest.

21. Vindiciae 4, 1 (ODW I, 405)
22. Storia delle Eresie, Confutazione 11, 8, 75 (OON 8, 360; ODW II, 442).
23. John 13. 13.
24. John 14. 16 - 17.
25. Storia delle Eresie, Confutazione 11, 8, 76 (OON 8, 361; ODW II, 442).
26. Matthew 28. 20.
27. Storia delle Eresie, Confutazione 11, 8, 77 (OON 8, 361; ODW II, 443)
28. Ibid.
29. Storia delle Eresie, Confutazione 11, 8, 85 (OON 8, 363; ODW II, 446).
30. Ibid.
31. Storia delle Eresie
32. Verita della Fede 3, 10, 17 (OON 8, 218; ODW I, 354).
33. Vindiciae 7, 17 (ODW I, 439).
34. Vindiciae 9, 12 (ODW I, 451).
35. Ibid.
36. ASS 6, (1870) 321.

ABBREVIATIONS

AAS....... Acta Apostolicae Sedis

ACW...... Ancient Christian Writers

ASS....... Acta Sanctae Sedis

BRC...... Bullari Romani Continuatio

BR(T)..... Bullarum, Diplomatum et Privilegiorum sanctorum Romanorum Pontificum Tauriensis editio

CC......... Corpus Christianorum

CE......... Catholic Encyclopedia

CJC....... Corpus Juris Canonicis

CL......... Collectio Lacensis

CSEL..... Corpus Scriptorum Ecclesiasticorum Latinorum

CTSA..... Proceedings of the Catholic Theological Society of America

DAFC..... Dictionnaire Apologetique de la foi Catholique

DE......... Dizionario Ecclesiastico

DTC...... Dictionnaire de Theologie Catholique

EC . . . . Enciclopedia Cattolica

LL . . . . Letters of St. Alphonsus de Liguori

LTK . . . . . . Lexikon fur Theologie und Kirche

Mansi . . . . . Sacrorum Conciliorum nova et amplissima Collectio

MBR . . . . . . Magnum Bullarium Romanorum

ODW . . . . . . Opera Dogmatica Sancti Alphonsi, ed. by A. Walter.

OMG . . . . . . Opera Moralia Sancti Alphonsi, ed. by L. Gaude

OON . . . . . . Opere di S. Alfonso de Liguori

OOS . . . . Bellarmine Omnia Opera, ed. by X. Sforza

OOV . . . . . . Suarez, Omnia Opera, Vives edition

PG . . . . Patrologiae Cursus Completus, Series Graeca

PL . . . . Patrologiae Cursus Completus, Series Latina

BIBLIOGRAPHY

GENERAL EDITIONS OF THE WORKS OF ST. ALPHONSUS

Letters of St. Alphonsus M. de Ligouri 5 vols. tr. by E. Grimm (New York, 1891 - 1897).

Opere Ascetiche, vol. 1 - (Rome, 1933).

Opere di S. Alfonso M. de Liguori, vol. 8 Opere Dommatiche (Naples, 1871)

Opera Dogmatica 2 vols. edited by A. Walter (Rome, 1903).

Opera Moralia 4 vols. edited by L. Gaude (Rome, 1905 - 1912).

INDIVIDUAL WRITINGS OF ST. ALPHONSUS

Breve dissertazione contro gli errori de moderni Increduli, oggidi nominati materialisti e deisti. (OON 8, 1 - 30; ODW I, 5 -31).

Dissertatio de justa prohibitione et abolitione librorum nocuae lectionis brevi calamo plura continens quae diffuse ab auctoribus tradita sunt. (OMG I, 253 - 291).

Dissertatio de Romani Pontificis auctoritate super propositionem 29 damnatam ab Alexandro VIII, quae dicebat: Futilis et toties convulsa est

assertio de Pontificis Romani supra concilium oecumenicum auctoritate atque in fidei quaestionibus decernendis infallibilitate.
(OMG I, 93 - 121).

Dissertazione Theologiche-Morali appartenenti alla vita eterna.
(OON 8, 1 - 76; ODW II, 535 - 627).

Evidenza della Fede, ossia Verita della Fede, fatta evidente per li contrassegni della sua credibilita.
(OON 8, 1 - 45; ODW I, 43 - 84)

Opera dommatica contro gli Eretici pretesi riformati.
(OON 8, 1 - 211; ODW I, 465 - 717).

Trionfo della Chiesa, ossia Istoria delle Eresie colle lore confutazione.
(OON 8, 1 - 425; ODW II, 1 - 503).

Verita della Fede contro i materialisti che negano l'esistenza di Dio, i deisti che negano la religione rivelata, ed i Settari che negano la Chiesa cattolica essere l'unica vera.
(OON 8, 1 - 245; ODW I, 99 - 378).

Vindiciae pro Suprema Romani Pontificis Potestate adversus Justinum Febronium, opella ab Honorio de Honoriis elucubrata.
(ODW I, 383 - 459).

OTHER COLLECTED SOURCES

Acta Apostolicae Sedis, vol. 1 - (Rome, 1909-).

Acta Gregorii PP XVI, vol. 2 (Rome, 1901)

Acta Sanctae Sedis, vol. 1 - (Rome, 1865 -)

Bullarum, Diplomatum et Privilegiorum sanctorum Romanorum Pontificium Tauriensis editio, tome 1 - (Turin, 1857 -)

Bullari Romani Continuatio, tome 1 - (Rome, 1835 -)

Collectio Lacensis, Acta et decreta Sacrorum Conciliorum Recentium, tome 1 - (Freiburg, 1870 -)

Corpus Christianorum, vol. 1 - (Brepols, 1954 -).

Corpus Juris Canonicis, 2 vols. (Leipsig, 1879).

Corpus Scriptorum Ecclesiasticorum Latinorum, editum consilio Academiae Litterarum Caesereae, vol. 1 - (Vienna, 1866 -).

Jaffe, P. Regesta Pontificum Romanorum, vol. 1 (Berlin, 1851).

Magnum Bullarium Romanum, vol. 1 - (Luxembourgh, 1727 -).

Mansi, J. Sacrorum Conciliorum nova et amplissima Collectio vol. 1 - (Florence, 1759 - afterwards, Paris and Leipsig)

Minge, J. Patrologiae Cursus Completus, Series Graeca, vol. 1 - (Paris, 1857 -).

--------- Patrologiae Cursus Completus, Series Latina, vol. 1 - (Paris, 1844 -).

REFERENCE WORKS

Agius, G. Tradition and the Church (Boston, 1928)

Alexander, N. Historia Ecclesiastica, 9 tomes (Luca, 1734).

Altaner, A. Patrologie (Freiburg, 1950).

Amann, E. "Nicolas I" DTC 11/1 (L931) 506 - 526.

---------- "Sarpi" DTC 14 (1939) 1115 - 1121

Arnauld, A. Oeuvres Completes, vols. 17 & 19 (Paris, 1783).

Arquilliere, H. "L'appel au concile sous Philippe le Bel" Revue des Questions Historiques 45 (1911) 23 - 55.

---------- "L'origin des theories conciliares" Seances et Travaux de l'Academie des Sciences Morales et Politiques 175 (1911) 573 - 586.

Aubenas, R. "Le Pontificat de Jules II et les debuts de Leon X" in Fliche-Martin, Histoire de L'Eglise 15 (Paris, 1951) 151 - 201.

Aubert, R. Le Pontificat de Pie IX, Fliche-Martin, Histoire de L'Eglise 20 (Paris, 1952).

Augustine, St. Enarrationem in Psalmum 108, CC 40 (1954).

Bardenhewer, O. Patrology, tr. by J. Shahan (St. Louis, 1908).

Bardy, G. "Sozomene" DTC 14/2 (1941) 2469 - 2471.

Baudrillart, A. "Bale (Concile de)" DTC 2/1 (1932) 113 - 129.

----------- "Constance (Concile de)" DTC 3/1 (1938) 1197 - 1124.

Baylon, R. Como Escribio S. Alfonso de Ligorio (Madrid, 1950).

Bazzi, P. Tanucci" Dizionario Ecclesiastico 3 (1958) 1726 - 1735.

Becano, M. Controversia Angelicana (Mainz, 1612).

Becque, M. Le Cardinal Dechamps 2 vols. (Louvain, 1956).

Bellarmine, R. Card. St. Opera Omnia vols. 1 & 2 (Naples, 1856 - 1857).

Bellia, S. Chiesa e Stato nel Pensiero di L. Sturzo (Rome, 1956).

Bernard, E. "Doctrinal Value of the Ordinary Teaching of the Holy Father" CTSA (1951) 78 - 107.

Bernard, St. De Consideratione PL, 182.

Berthe, A. Life of St. Alphonsus M. de Ligouri 2 vols. tr. by H. Castle (Dublin, 1905).

Bevenot, M. "Primatus Petro datur St. Cyprian on the Papacy" Journal of Theological Studies n.s. 5 (1954) 9 - 35.

---------- St. Cyprian, the Lapsed, the Unity of the Catholic Church in Quasten-Plumpe, Ancient Christian Writers 25 (Westminster, 1957).

Billot, L. Tractatus de Ecclesia Christi (Rome, 1927).

Burghardt, W. "The Catholic Concept of Tradition in the Light of Modern Theological Thought" CTSA (1951) 42 - 75.

Burke, E. "The Scientific Teaching of Theology in the Seminary" CTSA (1949) 129 - 173.

Buschi, E. Sant' Alfonso e il Papa (Pisano, 1933).

Butler, E. "The Catholic Church and Modern European Civilization" in Eyre, European Civilization, its Origins and Developments vol. 6 (Oxford, 1937).

Cacciatore, G. "Alfonso Maria de Ligouri" Enciclopedia Cattolica 1 (1948).

---------- Saint Alfonso de Ligouri e il Giansenismo (Florence, 1944).

Cano, M. De Locis Theologicis (Salamanca, 1563).

Cantu, C. Storia Universale vol. 10 (Turin, 1889).

Capasso, B. Sulla Circoscrizione Civile de Ecclesiastica e sulla Popolazione della Citta di Napoli (Naples, 1882).

Carreyre, J. "Jansenisme" DTC 8/1 (1947) 319 - 529.

---------- "Launoy" DTC 9/1 (1926) 2 - 6.

---------- "Maimbourg" DTC 9/2 (1927) 1656 - 1661.

---------- "Pistoe (Synode de)" DTC 12/2 (1935) 2134 - 2230.

Casel, O. "Eine missverstandene Stelle Cyprians" Revue Benedictine 30 (1913) 413 - 420.

Cavalerra, F. Thesaurus Doctrinae Ecclesiae (Paris, 1936).

Chapman, J. "Les interpolations dans le traite de S. Cyprien sur l'unite de l'Eglise" Revue Benedictine 19 (1902) 246 - 254; 357 - 373.

Choupin, L. Valeur des decisions du Saint Siege (Paris, 1912).

Coletta, P. Storia del Reame di Napoli (Milan, 1861).

Concessionis Tituli Doctoris in honorem S. Alphonsi M. de Ligorio 2 Tomes (Rome, 1870).

Congar, M. "Theologie" DTC 15/1 (1946) 342 - 502.

Conglio, G. "Tanucci" Enciclopedia Cattolica 11 (1954) 1735 - 1736.

Corrigan, R. The Church and the Nineteenth Century (Milwaukee, 1938).

Croce, B. Storia del Regno de Napoli (Bari, 1931).

---------- Uomini e Cose della Vecchia Italia vol. 2 (Bari, 1927).

D'Aguesseau, H. Oeuvres de M. le Chancelier d'Aguesseau vol. 13 (Paris, 1759).

D'Aguirre, J. Auctoritas infallibilis et summa Cathedrae S. Petri (Salamanca, 1683).

Declareuil, M. Histoire General du Droit Francaise (Paris, 1925).

Deikmann, H. De Ecclesia vol. 2 (Freibourg, 1925).

De Meulemeester, M. Bibliographie Generale des Ecrivains Redemptoristes 3 vols. (Louvain, 1933 - 1939).

---------- Outline History of the Redemptorists tr. by J. Gredler (Louvain, 1956).

De Vio, T. (Card. Cajetan) De Comparatione Auctoritatis Papae et Concilii (Rome, 1936).

Dublanchy, E. "Infallibilite de Pape" DTC 7/2 (1927) 1638 - 1717.

Dubruel, M. "Gallicanisme" DTC 6/1 (1947) 1096 - 1107.

Dubruel, M.-Arquilliere, H. "Gallicanisme" DAFC 2 (1912) 193 - 274.

Duval, A. Libelli de Ecclesiastica et publica Potestate (Paris, 1612).

---------- Libelli de Suprema Romani Ponticis in Ecclesia Potestate (Paris, 1614).

Ehrhard, A. Die Kirche der Martyrer (Munich, 1932).

Figgis, J. From Gerson to Grotius (Cambridge, 1916).

Franzelin, J. Card. De Ecclesia Christi (Rome, 1877).

---------- Tractatus de Divini Traditione et Scriptura (Rome, 1882).

Godet, P. "Gelase I" DTC 6/1 (1947) 1179-1180.

Gonsalez, T. De Infallibilitate Romani Pontificis (Rome, 1683).

Goodwin, C. (Sister) Papal Conflict with Josephism (New York, 1938).

Haering, B.-Zettl, "Alfons Maria di Ligouri" Lexikon fur Theologie und Kirche 1 (1957).

Hayes, C. History of Modern Europe, vol. 1 (New York, 1939).

Hefele-Leclercq, Histoire des Conciles vol. 7/2 (Paris, 1916).

Hughes, P. A History of the Church, 3 vols. (New York 1, 1948; 2, 1952; 3, 1947).

Ireneus, St. Adversus Haeresus PG 7.

Jacques, J. Du Pape et du Concile (Tournai, 1869).

Jamin, Dom N. Pensees Theologiques Relatives aux Erreurs du Temps, (Paris, 1792).

Jansen, J. Testimonia de S. Alfonso de Ligorio (Wittem, 1928).

Jemolo, A. Il Giansenismo in Italia prima Rivoluzione (Bari, 1925).

---------- Stato e Chiesa negli Scrittori Italiani del Seicento e del Settecento (Turin, 1914).

Jerome, St."Epistola 15 ad Damasum," CSEL 54.

Le Bachelet, X. "Alexandre VIII" DTC 1 (1930) 751.

Lecler, J. The Two Sovereignties (New York, 1952).

Lejay, P. "Dupin" Catholic Encyclopedia 5, 204 - 205.

Le Moyne, J. "S. Cyprien est-il bien l'auteur de la redaction breve du De Unitate Chaptier 4?" Revue Benedictine 63 (1953) 70 - 115.

Leo the Great, St. Sermo 4 & 51, PL 54

Lupus, J. Divinum ac immobile S. Petri... Privilegium Opera Omnia, vol. 8 (Venice, 1729).

Martin, V. "Comment s'est formee la doctrine de la Superiorite du concile sur le Pape" Revue des Sciences Religieuses 17 (1937) 121 - 143; 261 - 289; 414 - 427.

---------- Origines du Gallicanisme 2 vols. (Paris, 1939).

Michel A. "Tradition" DTC 15/1 (1946) 1252 - 1350.

Mourret, F. Le Concile du Vatican (Paris, 1919).

Nicalau, M.-Salaverri, J. Sacrae Theologiae Summa vol. 1 (Madrid, 1950).

Nicholas I, St. Epistola ad Michaelem Imperatorem Mansi, 15.

Nicolini, F. Le Teorie Politiche di Pietro Giannone (Naples, 1915).

Ortolan, T. "Febronianisme" DTC 5/2 (1939) 2115 - 2124.

Pastor, L. History of the Popes from the Close of the Middle Ages vol. 1 - (St. Louis, 1907 -), vols. 31 & 32, tr. by E. Graf; vols. 36 & 39 tr. by E. Peeler.

Pesch, C. Praelectiones Dogmaticae vol. 1 (Freibourg, 1924).

Petit-Didier, Dom M. De Auctoritate et Infallibilitate Summi Pontificis in Migne, Theologiae Cursus Completa 4.

Preclin, E. Les Jansenistes du XVIII Siecle et la Constitution Civile du Clerge (Paris, 1929).

Preclin, E.-Jarry, E. Les Luttes Politiques et Doctrinales aux XVIIe et XVIIIe Siecle in Fliche-Martin, Histoire de L'Eglise, 19/1 & 2 (Paris, 1955).

Quasten, J. Patrology 2 vols. (1, Brussels, 1950; 2, Westminister, 1953).

Rocaberti, J. De Romani Pontificis Auctoritate (Valencia, 1691 - 94).

Roverio, P., Demonstrationes vol. 2 (Lyons, 1616).

Ruggiero, G. Il Pensiero Politico Meridionale nei Secoli XVIII e XIX (Bari, 1946).

Salembier, L. "Gerson" DTC 6/1 (1947) 1313 - 1332.

Sampers, A. "Bibliographia Alfonsiana 1938 - 1953" Spicilegium Historicum 1 (1953) 248 - 271.

Sarpi, P. Istoria del Concilio Tridentino (London, 1619).

Schaff, P. Nicene and Post-Nicene Fathers, 2nd Series, vol. 2 (New York, 1890).

Schipa, M. Il Regno di Napoli sotto i Boboni (Naples, 1900).

Sfondrati, C. Card. Gallia Vindicata (Mantua, 1710).

Sozomen, S. Ecclesiastical History tr. by C. Hartranft in Nicene and Post-Nicene Fathers, 2nd Series, vol. 2 (New York, 1890) 181 - 454.

Sturzo, L. Church and State, tr. by B. Carter (London, 1939).

---------- Nationalism and Internationalism (New York, 1946).

Suarez, Opera Omnia, tome 12 (Paris, Vives, 1873).

Tannoia, A. Della Vita ed Istituto del Ven. S. di Dio, Alfonso M. de Ligouri 3 vols. (Naples, 1798 - 1802).

Telleria, R. Alfonso M. de Ligorio 2 vols.
(Madrid, 1950 - 51).

Tertullian, Scorpiace, CC 2 (1954)

Thomas Acquinas, St. Opera Omnia tome 1 -
(Parma, 1852 -)

Tierney, B. Foundations of the Conciliar Theory
(Cambridge, 1955).

Tin, E. "Doctrine de S. Alphonse de Ligouri
sur le pouvair Supreme et Infallibile de Pontife
Romaine" unpublished diss. Angelicum (Rome,
1953).

Ullman, W. Origins of the Great Schism (London, 1948).

Vacant, J. Etudes Theologiques sur les Constitutions du Concile du Vatican 2 vols. (Paris,
1895).

Von Hontheim, N. Justini Febronii Juris consulti de Statu Ecclesiae et legitima potestate Romani Pontificis liber singularis ad reuniendos dissidentes in religione Christiana compositus, (Bologna, 1765).

Weigel, G. "Commentaries on Humani Generis"
Theological Studies 12 (1952) 520 - 549.

Wernz, F.-Vidal, P. Jus Canonicum, vol. 2
(Rome, 1938).

Zapalena, T. De Ecclesia, vol. 2 (Rome, 1954).

TABLE OF CONTENTS
OF COMPLETE DISSERTATION

FOREWORD

ABBREVIATIONS

CHAPTER ONE
    AN HISTORICAL BACKGROUND TO THE WRITINGS OF SAINT ALPHONSUS ON PAPAL AUTHORITY

CHAPTER TWO
    THE WRITINGS OF SAINT ALPHONSUS ON PAPAL AUTHORITY

CHAPTER THREE
    SAINT ALPHONSUS' CONCEPT OF PAPAL AUTHORITY

CHAPTER FOUR
    PAPAL AUTHORITY IN SACRED SCRIPTURE ACCORDING TO THE TEACHING OF SAINT ALPHONSUS

CHAPTER FIVE
    SAINT ALPHONSUS' USE OF THE MAGISTERIUM TO ESTABLISH PAPAL AUTHORITY

Part I: An evaluation of Saint Alphonsus' use of the Magisterium

Part II: The teaching on Papal Authority Drawn from the Testimony of the Magisterium

CHAPTER SIX
> THE TEACHING OF SAINT ALPHONSUS ON PAPAL AUTHORITY DRAWN FROM THE FATHERS AND THEOLOGIANS

CHAPTER SEVEN
> SAINT ALPHONSUS' DEFENSE OF PAPAL POWER FROM THE ARGUMENTS OF HUMAN REASON

BIBLIOGRAPHY